Alcatraz:
The Last Survivors

Jon Forsling

ISBN-10: 1977985270
ISBN-13: 978-1977985279

This book is dedicated to my father

CONTENTS

Jon Forsling

INTRODUCTION

"Why do you write a book about Alcatraz?" prisoner number 935-AZ asks me later on in this book.

As I pondered an answer, my mind went back to an old memory of childhood.

I'm 11 years old and lying on a thin mattress on the living room floor of a single-story apartment located at 1925 San Antonio Avenue in Berkeley, California. Everyone is asleep. I can't sleep. I lie staring at a picture of three corpses.

Earlier in the day, my family and I had been to Alcatraz. Although I grew up in rural Sweden, this was not my first visit to the Bay Area as a kid – nor would it be my last. The reason for this was that my dad was an exchange student at the University of California at Berkeley in the early 1960's and kept in touch with the woman he rented a room from. Her name was Ruth Huenemann and she had no children of her own, so once every four or five years she would bring us over to stay with her for a week or two. These trips were probably my happiest childhood memories, which played a part in my later obsession with the subject of this book.

During my first visit to "The Rock" I was given a thin pamphlet about the fourteen escape attempts that were made from the federal prison. Men who drowned. Men who were shot in the head, or executed.

And – in an image that was especially gruesome – three men who died after a 40-hour long shoot-out, their naked bodies lying on a bunk in the San Francisco morgue. Marvin Hubbard. Bernard Coy. Joe Cretzer. They all chose death over captivity. I saw something heroic in this, and the three dead prisoners instantly became my heroes.

Or anti-heroes, perhaps. My personal rebels.

This was in February 1986. A few days later the phone rang. A neighbor of Ruth's had seen on television that the Swedish prime minister Olof Palme had been shot dead in Stockholm. It was big news, even in the United States, and we sat glued to the television and radio throughout the evening. My mother cried. When we flew home the next day, Sweden felt paralyzed and dazed, our fellow citizens walking around in a trance-like state and blinking as if in surprise towards the daylight.

On Monday, at school in Tärnsjö – the little sleepy village where I grew up – I burst of eagerness to tell the class about my U.S. trip. But our teacher couldn't care less about my adventure. We observed a minute of silence for our fallen prime minister, and then he told us to draw paintings in his honor which were later sent to the local daily *Sala Allehanda* newspaper.

So, Alcatraz remained my secret. Over the years, my interest in the island grew into a passion.

Then, an obsession.

I wrote short stories and songs about certain, tragic prisoners who tried to escape but failed: Thomas Limerick (who murdered a guard in '38 and was later shot dead), Aaron Burgett (who drowned in '58), "Doc" Barker (who was shot dead in '39) and Sam Shockley (who was executed in '48). Together with my friend Henke, I began to carve a hole in the cement wall of a toilet in our secondary school in Östervåla to try to recreate Frank Morris and the Anglin brothers' famous escape in 1962. We didn't get as far as they did.

I bought a turtle and named it Morris. He died after a few weeks.

One day I looked out over the fields of northern Uppland through the window of my childhood home and started crying when I thought of John Giles, a prisoner who planned an escape for several years only to find himself being caught after about 15 minutes. The memory is crystal clear, even thirty years later: how a huge wave of empathy – for a man I did not know and would never meet – suddenly washed over me as if from nowhere.

As an adult, I continued to hunt the island like a fox after a mechanical rabbit. Time after time (six, if I remember correctly), I flew to San Francisco and took the ferry over to the island. I have devoured book after book after book about the prison. In my job as a freelance journalist, I have written article after article about the island in Swedish newspapers until my editors have started rolling their eyes and calling me crazy.

The only thing that was left to do with my obsession was to write a book. The idea to seek out and interview the last surviving prisoners began to take shape at the beginning of 2016. The year before, I had gone to San Francisco and wrote a series of articles for the Swedish daily *Aftonbladet*, where – among other things – I met the then 88-year-old ex-prisoner Bob Luke. It struck me that there must be very few others like Bob remaining today; the prison closed over half a century ago, after all. After thorough research – with help from the staff of the National Park Service, which today operates Alcatraz as a museum – I concluded that there were less than 20 prisoners still living, out of a total of 1,545[1] who served time on the island. That number does not include the three prisoners who escaped in 1962 – although there is. of course, a small chance that one or all of them

---

[1] The last prisoner number issued was 1576, but several inmates received more than one number.

may also be alive. A very small group of people, in other words, that in a few years will be completely decimated.

The idea emerged to write a book about these last survivors, and — based on their stories — create a "requiem" of sorts for the world's most notorious prison.

I started calling, e-mailing and writing letters to old men that were living all over the mainland U.S. (and one in Puerto Rico). Some were easy to locate; others called for a certain amount of detective work. Some did not respond to my requests, but nine agreed to share their life stories. Some had been free men for decades; others were still behind bars. One had found God; others were convinced atheists. Some remembered their years at Alcatraz in detail; others had repressed them.

Why did Alcatraz put its claws into me that winter day in 1986 — and why has the solitary island not yet let go of its grip? I cannot give a simple answer to that question.

Maybe the prison, over the years, has become a symbol of the loneliness and confusion I often feel in life. And perhaps that confusion affects all of us sometimes. Every one of us, after all, is isolated on our own, private island. All of us can probably relate to the feeling of being trapped in an exercise yard and looking out over green waves and a beautiful, red suspension bridge.

And wishing we could be there, instead of here.

— Jon Forsling, Västerås, Sweden, in the summer of 2018

ALCATRAZ: 1934-1963

The mist rises from San Francisco Bay at dawn and settles like a wraith between the island and the sleeping city. In the morning, the day's first ferry leaves the dock from Pier 33 on Fisherman's Wharf. The green salt water whips its gunwale. Beyond the bow, an island slowly appears like a warship in the thick haze. Then the veils of mist disperse, and there it is:

Devil's Island.

"The Rock."

Hellcatraz.

They say a child that is loved goes by many different names.

So does a child that is feared.

***

At first glance, it is still difficult to understand what it was that so frightened generations of American mobsters. With an area of just over 89,000 square meters, Alcatraz is a small island. The landscape is peaceful but barren, and the prison – once so feared and awe-inspiring – today looks rather sad and forlorn. The white-painted concrete has yellowed with age and is crumbling in places. A stillness descends over the empty cell house and the deserted yard when the tourists have gone home for the day. At night, Alcatraz is now quiet like a tomb, which is fitting – soon, there will be no one left alive that can remember the prison when it was active. This is a book about the last survivors of that era. But first, let us go back to the beginning of it all.

To the year 1859, to be exact.

Alcatraz was only inhabited by birds before that. The island's name evolved from "La Isla de los Alcatraces" ("Pelican Island"), as it was called in 1775 by the Spanish naval officer Juan de Ayala, when he was among the first to explore San Francisco Bay. But in 1859 the U.S. Army settled itself on Alcatraz Island. Because of the island's strategic location – only about a mile from the San Francisco harbor – they built a fort on Alcatraz as protection against foreign invaders. These invaders never came, and in 1909 the military leadership realized that the island was suited for a different purpose. The Army needed a new prison. San Francisco Bay – with its treacherous currents constantly moving out toward the Pacific Ocean – functioned as an insurmountable wall.

Led by Major Reuben Turner, construction began of a rectangular, ultramodern colossus of concrete that housed four cell blocks, a kitchen, a dining room, a library, a hospital, a shower room – all under one roof. To accommodate 600 men, the cells in cell blocks A, B and C were made claustrophobically small, measuring 1.5 x 2.5 meters. The isolation cells in cell block D were slightly larger, because they were reserved for the unruliest prisoners who would have to sit in them around the clock. The prison building was finished in 1912, but it would be many more years before Alcatraz became known as Devil's Island. During the following two decades, the island was home to deserters and Army prisoners. Harmless men – compared to the hardened criminals that would soon populate the tiny cells.

When the stock markets crashed in 1929, a new kind of lawlessness began to take hold in the United States. Organized crime gangs took advantage of the subsequent poverty and mass unemployment during The Great Depression to spread their tentacles into every corner of society. Stylishly dressed, sadistic bosses soon ruled huge crime syndicates that threatened to take over entire cities. Police were powerless to stop this development. They blacklisted the most powerful criminals and called them "Public Enemies," but that only made mythological figures out of men like Al Capone, "Pretty

Boy" Floyd and "Machine Gun" Kelly. To be a gangster in the 1930´s was to be a folk hero of sorts.

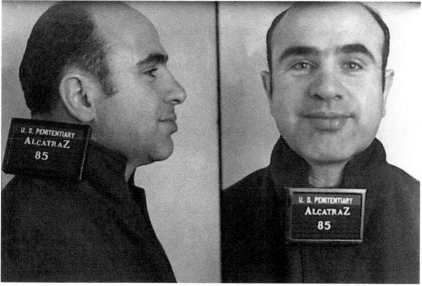

Al Capone, 85-AZ

At the FBI head office in Washington, D.C., the young director J. Edgar Hoover came up with a plan. He had heard of a small military prison on an island in San Francisco Bay that could fit his purposes. At the end of 1933 he decided – with the backing of Attorney General Homer Cummings and the director of the Federal Bureau of Prisons, Sanford Bates – that it was time to fight fire with fire. When Alcatraz was transferred to federal ownership on Jan. 1, 1934, Hoover fed the press stories of how strict the routines would be in the new super prison: How impossible it would be to escape; how tightly the prisoners would be maintained; how few privileges they would get. The symbolism of this was as important as the prison itself. By creating a grim counterpoint to America's glamorous criminal elite, J. Edgar Hoover sent a warning to the powerful mafia and a message to a crime-weary American public: *No one is above the law. This is the ultimate destination for those who choose lawlessness and anarchy.* The first prisoners arrived in leg-irons on Aug. 11, 1934. Eleven days later, the leader of the mob in Chicago, and one of America's most infamous criminals, joined them. Al "Scarface" Capone was accustomed to handing out orders, but when he stepped off the gangplank with swollen ankles, he left his tyrant status back on the mainland. On the island, he was 85-AZ, nothing more. Another faded denim shirt in the crowd. Another world-famous gangster, George "Machine Gun" Kelly, soon joined him as prisoner number 117-AZ. For the following 29 years, Alcatraz reduced America's most dangerous men to numbers. Over 1,500 men did hard time on Alcatraz. The last prisoner to receive a registration number before the prison closed in March 1963, Frank Weatherman, was number 1576-AZ.

***

Alcatraz was meant to be escape-proof – a sort of prison equivalent of the unsinkable ship *Titanic* – but that did not stop a total of 36 prisoners from trying. Their names and tragic fates were whispered with a mixture of fear and respect from prisoner to prisoner in the drafty cell house:

Joe Bowers, who was shot dead as he tried to climb a fence in 1936.

Ted Cole and Ralph Roe, who managed to get down to the water's edge but were spotted drowning by several witnesses in 1937.

Rufus "Whitey" Franklin, Jimmy Lucas and Thomas Limerick, who killed a guard in 1938 and went up on the roof of the prison. There, they tried to storm one of the guard towers, but before they could reach it another guard opened fire on them. Limerick was shot dead, Lucas gave up, Franklin was hit and injured and had to spend the next 14 years in solitary confinement.

Arthur "Doc" Barker, a former public enemy and a member of the notorious Karpis/Barker gang, who in 1939 was among five prisoners who managed to saw out of their cells in cell block D in the middle of the night, then made it as far as the beach. Four gave up; one was injured; Barker was shot in the head. His last words: "I was an idiot for trying. Now I'm totally shot to hell."

James Boarman: shot in the head as he and three fellow inmates struggled in the waves after having overpowered a guard and climbed a fence in 1943. The other three gave up. Boarman died.

And then there was the story of the spectacular "Battle of Alcatraz" in 1946, when six prisoners got hold of door keys and firearms and took several guards hostage. When they realized the prison was surrounded, three of them gave up and returned to their cells. But the most desperate of the prisoners, a 35-year old bank robber named Joe Cretzer, started executing the captive guards instead. Then he barricaded himself, with two fellow prisoners Bernard Coy and Marvin Hubbard, in a narrow utility corridor behind cell block C. After more than 40 hours, U.S. Marines managed to gain entrance into the hallway and killed the three men. When the smoke had dispersed, two guards were dead and 11 others were wounded. Two of the three prisoners who had given up – Sam Shockley and Miran Thompson – were later executed at San Quentin for their roles in the drama. The third one – 19-year-old Clarence Carnes – was allowed to live, partly because of his youth.

Joe Cretzer, 548-AZ

Fatal escape attempts mainly occurred during the prison's first 12 years of existence. After the "Battle of Alcatraz" in 1946, only one other prisoner is known to have died during an escape attempt: Aaron Burgett, who drowned in 1958. What happened to the three men who disappeared without a trace in 1962 is – and will likely always be – unknown. The "Battle of Alcatraz" had an immense impact on the prison. Prison authorities slowly began to loosen the suffocating restrictions in the late 1940's, under pressure from a public horrified by the bloody events of 1946:

"Alcatraz wasn't the same place after the riot," says ex-inmate Harvey Carignan (935-AZ), who arrived on the island in 1951.

"The public learned a lot about the prison because of the riot, and it was inevitable that it had to change for the better – which the warden and the guards didn't like. I came to Alcatraz five years after the riot, and got to know many prisoners who had been there before the incident. And they all said that the rules had been relaxed a bit after the "Battle of Alcatraz", which made it somewhat more tolerable to do time there."

***

The myth of Alcatraz as a cruel and inhuman hell-hole has been cultivated by the media and Hollywood over the years. It is both an exaggerated and simplified description of the prison, but it makes the island perfectly suited to play the cultural role of Goliath in a world full of nuances and shades of gray between good and evil.

But there is no doubt that it *could* be a deadly place. During the prison's history, eight prisoners were murdered by other prisoners, and at least ten more died trying to escape. In addition, five prisoners committed suicide, and 15 prisoners died of what were classified as "natural causes." And Alcatraz did have aspects that were sadistic, bordering on torture. In the 1930s, all inmates were forced to be completely silent when they were locked in their cells, which meant total solitude for at least 15 hours a day. This, combined with the claustrophobia of being locked in such small cells, led some to lose their sanity.

The harshest place on "The Rock" was the notorious so-called "hole" – a dark cell in cell block D used to punish inmates who broke the rules. For up to 19 days at a time (or 29 or even 90, according to two of the prisoners in this book), naked prisoners were confined to the pitch-black darkness of a cold and empty cell. Pretty soon they lost both temporal and spatial orientation, but their cries for mercy fell on deaf ears.

Movies about Alcatraz often feature exceedingly brutal guards, something that is not rooted in reality. But sadistic prison guards make for a better story. Pop culture is full of cases where Alcatraz has been reduced to either a menacing backdrop – as in purely fictional films such as "The Rock" (1996), "X-Men: The Last Stand" (2006) and "The Book of Eli" (2010) – or as the incarnation of pure evil, such as in the 1994 movie "Murder in the First", which grotesquely distorted a true event from 1941 in which a prisoner (Henri Young, 244-AZ) murdered another prisoner (Rufus McCain, 267-AZ). "Murder in the First" shamelessly plundered every prison film cliché available. Tyrannical guards? Check. Underground cellars? Check. Innocently condemned prisoner, with a halo over his head? Yep, that too.

This is also why Clint Eastwood (in a cowboy-tough portrayal of Frank Morris) struggles not only against walls and bars but also against a sadistic warden in what is perhaps the best movie ever made about the prison, "Escape from Alcatraz" (1979). Here, the cruel warden cliché is both unnecessary and untrue – in reality, the warden at the time of the escape, Olin Blackwell, was a well-liked man. A strictly factual depiction of the escape would have been compelling enough without any fictional embellishments.

As Bob Luke, prisoner 1118-AZ, puts it:

"The first thing one can say is that Alcatraz was not like the movies. Take Clint Eastwood's "Escape from Alcatraz" for example. There were never any naked prisoners walking around in the cell house, and you could sit wherever you wanted on the steps in the yard. They described the escape pretty good, but nothing else." Alcatraz will likely go down in history as the epitome of a cruel and harsh prison. The prisoners in this book remember it that way, but for more subtle afflictions than the ones dramatized by Hollywood. The worst part, they say, was the deadly monotony that prevailed on the island. Alcatraz was a place flooded with rules and procedures, and the slightest infringement of these rules would be met by swift, severe retribution.

At 06:33, a gong sounded in the cell house. Twelve minutes later, all prisoners had to be standing upright by the bars – clean, shaven and dressed – to be counted by the guards. Those who didn't comply went without breakfast and got a reprimand. If it happened again, a prisoner would find himself in an isolation cell in cell block D.

At 06:55, the cell doors opened, and the prisoners marched in straight, orderly lines to eat their breakfast. The dining room looked like a small, airplane hangar – a long, rectangular room where it always seemed to be either dusk or dawn because the daylight was heavily filtered by thick window grilles. Here the men ate three well-prepared and nutritious meals a day, food whose high standards surprised many who had expected something like bread and water in America's toughest prison.

Tear-gas canisters hung from the ceiling to prevent fights, and guards patrolled outside the windows carrying Springfield rifles. The men got exactly 20 minutes to eat everything on their plate. The cutlery was counted both before and after each meal. If a knife or fork went missing, the prison shut down until the guilty thief came forward. Then came eight hours of work, with a break for lunch. The prisoners were divided into small groups and trudged off to their workplaces under close surveillance by the guards. Scattered across the island were workshops where the men – for a paltry pay rate of 20 to 30 cents an hour – made furniture, rugs, various items of clothing, and leather gloves, on behalf of the U.S. Army. Other possible jobs to choose from were chef (one of the most coveted jobs), cleaner (not as desirable), librarian, gardener, painter and barber.

At 16:25 the prisoners returned to the dining room for twenty minutes of dinner. At 16:45 they all marched back to their cells. There they remained; until the next morning. The lights in the cell house's roof went out at 21:30, and the men would be counted during the night in their cells at 00:01, 03:00 and 05:00. In that fashion, hours slowly turned into days and weeks and years. But for many at Alcatraz, it was like the clocks had stopped working for good.

"It was a *very* boring place to do time," says ex-prisoner Bill Baker (1259-AZ).

***

Alcatraz was a federal prison for 29 years before it closed on March 21, 1963, on the orders of Attorney General Robert F. Kennedy. The official reason was that it was too expensive to keep running, but one of the prisoners in this book has a piquant, non-official theory about why Kennedy made the decision.

It is difficult to determine how effective the prison really was from a rehabilitation point of view. Other than for religious practices, there was no space for reflection and soul-searching on Alcatraz. It was, first and foremost, a storage place for incorrigible prisoners that other, "ordinary" prisons couldn't handle.

The men in this book may have committed long-ago offenses, but the crimes themselves are timeless and could just as well have been committed today: Rape and murder, various types of violent crimes, financial fraud, bank robberies – even an act of terrorism directed against the United States.

Of the nearly twenty prisoners who are still alive, three are behind bars as of this writing, and all three committed their most serious crimes long after they left Alcatraz. Another prisoner interviewed in this book, Bill Baker, was sent to Alcatraz at age 23 and then went in and out of various other prisons until he was 78 years old. For these men, Alcatraz was no final destination; rather, it was a milestone on a long journey through the bleak milieu of the federal penitentiary system.

And then there are prisoners like Bob Luke, Jerry Clymore, Charlie Hopkins and Bob Schibline, who managed to reverse their lives after Alcatraz and who have spent several decades as free family men.

But did Alcatraz rehabilitate them, or were they rehabilitated despite having been sent to the island? It seems to have been mostly happenstance that kept them straight. Bob Luke thanks his large family for helping him to get on his feet. Bob Schibline was thwarted from robbing more banks when his accomplice unexpectedly got caught and sent back to prison.

"There was no such thing as rehabilitation," he said to me. "Alcatraz was meant to break us, physically, mentally and spiritually."

Jerry Clymore (1339-AZ), who spent 30 years in a variety of institutions before finally being released in 1985, and who therefore knows what he's talking about, believes that Alcatraz should be taken as a relic of a bygone era, when prisons generally weren't meant to rehabilitate criminals.

"Until the 1980's, prison was a place of punishment," he told me. "In the 1980's, the Bureau of Prisons, state and federal, began to focus on rehabilitation. All kinds of programs were brought in. Religious programs, Alcoholics Anonymous, anger management, and various social programs."

For Jerry Clymore and many other Alcatraz inmates, "The Rock" was no turning point. Just an unusually cold and desolate haul.

***

Voices from a distant past come to life in this book. The world has in many ways moved on since Alcatraz operated. The same thing goes for the men who lived there.

By interviewing the last surviving prisoners, I hope to be able to demystify the island to a certain degree. Alcatraz today is more a legend than a real place, and when the last prisoners die, the mist of mythology will permanently settle itself over the large cell house. No longer will reality be able to oppose the clichéd image of "Hellcatraz," and the men who did time there will go down in memory as a nameless mass of evil monsters.

But here they are, one last time: people of flesh and blood, who long ago were locked up on a windswept island in San Francisco Bay, dreaming of freedom.

935-AZ

Harvey Carignan has done unspeakably vile things in his life.

Yet it's almost possible to feel sympathy for him. These days he is an imprisoned, harmless man, over 90 years old. He talks intelligently and vividly about religion, politics and philosophy, and often refers to various poets and writers who have touched him through the years.

Harvey has been incarcerated since I was two and a half months old. He will die in prison.

We started corresponding in the winter of 2016, and during the exchanging of pleasantries and amid talk about poetry I felt like an angler trying to reel in a monster fish: Who are you, Harvey? Where are you from? Is there an answer, or an explanation, or a beginning and an end, to your immense evil?

Harvey struggles and squirms. I have him on the hook, but he pulls free.

***

There is a letter in the mail. Five pages long, typed, well structured, comprehensive and carefully written – the way people corresponded in the old world before e-mail and Facebook and Twitter existed. But there are some numbers at the top that I do not understand:

40685 // January 13, 2016 // 06:45 pm CST

It turns out that Harvey Louis Carignan, aka "The Want-Ad Killer", aka "Harv the Hammer," indulges in a strange peculiarity. For 41 years, one of America's most vicious serial killers has counted all the letters that he sends from his cell in the Minnesota Correctional Facility in Faribault, Minnesota.

Dear Mr. Forsling,

Thank you for your letter of 3 January. (...) This is the 40685th letter I've written since my incarceration beginning back on September 25, 1974, and I am sure that I have received quite as many. I cannot keep them, and I most foolishly failed to keep a record of them such as I have the letters I have written. It would be such a boon to my memory, which is fading quickly so far as short-term subjects are concerned. I can remember my first day in school better than what I did yesterday. Three days ago, I hardly remember anything whatsoever.

Three pages later he concludes with an unusually heartfelt goodbye:

Take care, and may the force of all that is good be with you always,

Harvey

In September 1974, the decayed corpse of Eileen Hunley was found in Shelbourne County, Minnesota. Harvey Carignan had beaten her to death with a hammer. Before she died, he had raped her with a tree branch.

Carignan is convicted of a variety of rapes and of murdering two women, but he is suspected to have killed at least five women and possibly as many as 18. He committed his first murder in 1949, the last in 1974. His modus operandi was to seek out women using personal ads, and then hit them in the head with a hammer while he forced them to perform oral sex on him. The youngest of his victims was only 13 years old.

Harvey Carignan has previously claimed that he was performing God's work when he killed his victims, because they were "unclean."

Why did he claim that? The question hangs in my mind as I continue reading.

As you know, I have grown quite old. My birthday is May 15, 1926, although the official record shows it to be May 18, 1927. That was my brother's birth date. I was born a bastard in New York State (Hastings-on-the-Hudson, to be exact) and did not have a birth certificate. I was named Harley Lawrence Belanger-Walker after my parents' families I was later told, so when my brother Harvey Louis died at the age of 31 days, it was an opportunity too great to let pass. They gave me his name, birth name and place of birth, which was Fargo, North Dakota if what they told me was true.

Much of what I was told when I was young turned out to be false, but my grandmother had a birth/marriage/death book that had begun in 1602 in a place now called Nova Scotia, but was then French and was being run over by the British and all the residents were forced to flee. Some went to Philadelphia and others to the West Indies to Baton Rogue, Louisiana in 1837 and on up to Canada again in 1867.

I have no proof of this, but I was told by my great grandmother on my stepfather's side that her father had shot and killed another man from the family over a game of poker. The law officer, a forerunner of the Royal Canadian Mounted Police, had arrested him that same night, acted as a judge in his trial the day after and as hangman the day following that. True? I have no inkling, but it made a great story that I listened all agog and until recently believed it with all that was in me. Now, I do not know.

In her bestselling book "The Want-Ad Killer" from 1983, author Ann Rule wrote about Harvey Carignan's childhood in detail.

According to her, he was a short little boy who had tics, used to wet the bed, and had an imaginary friend named Paul. During his childhood he was an unwanted child who was passed back and forth between different relatives. At age 11 he began committing petty crimes and was sent to a juvenile detention center in North Dakota, where he was diagnosed with Huntington's disease, a hereditary neurological and neuropsychiatric disorder characterized by nervous twitching of the face, arms and legs.

According to Ann Rule, Harvey was sexually abused by female employees during his time in the detention center.

When he was 18, he enlisted in the Army and was sent to a military base in Anchorage, Alaska. It was there that he committed his first murder, in the summer of 1949. Harvey raped 57-year-old Laura Showalter and then beat her to death. He fled from the murder scene but was arrested two months later while attempting another rape.

Harvey was sentenced to death by hanging for the murder of Showalter. But the police in Anchorage made some bureaucratic mistakes during their investigation, and the penalty was converted to 15 years in prison for rape.

On Sept. 13, 1951, he arrived on Alcatraz to begin serving his sentence. Harvey was booked as inmate 935-AZ:

My time there was a long era of futility, but I did leave a smarter person than when I arrived. There were some very intelligent people there and I hung with them as much as possible, which was not for very long at a time: lock-in time forbade it. I knew people who learned to play musical instruments there, and who wrote tremendous stories under pseudonyms that may or may not have been published.

I myself learned the meaning of reading, to appreciate what they said and how to utilize the knowledge I gleaned from them. For instance, I "met" Ayn Rand through her writing, especially "The Fountainhead", and I also remember a book by a psychologist named Clymer whose books was "verboten" by the prison authorities. We disguised it as a Bible cover and passed it around from person to person. Clarence Carnes, a prisoner who worked in the library, was the instigator of this.

The day to day routine at Alcatraz was stifling. We left our cells in the morning to eat breakfast, returned to our cells and left for work. At noon we came back, went to our cells and were counted, and then went to lunch. After lunch we returned to our cells, and then went to work. I am not sure what time we came in from work, but we were counted in our cells, let out for supper, returned to our cells, were counted and locked in until the next morning.

After supper the MTA (medical technician's assistant) came by with the guard and poured aspirin into the cups of the inmates who wanted it. I never once took any nor was I asked nor cajoled to. I soon became someone to pass by and not ask if I wanted any. I made their job easier from what I gleaned from this.

Sure, I was tempted to escape. Everyone I knew was tempted in one way or another, but that temptation is as far as it got. Common sense told me I would not make good at escaping, so I allowed the thought to die and sat back and did my time.

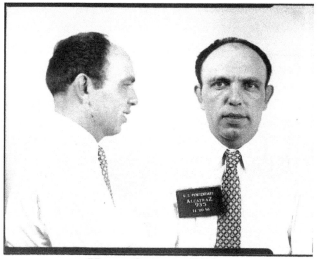

Harvey Carignan, 1956

I worked downstairs in the laundry at the end. Before that I had spent most of the time in the glove shop and tailor shop, but I heard that money was coming with every bunch of laundry from Fort Mason. I was getting short – had little time left to serve – and I wanted to see if I could get some. I did not. Those who were already working there had full control over it and were not letting it go, nor did I blame them! There were no hard feelings concerning that. If there was truly money coming in I never knew for certain and to this day do not.

During his time in the laundry Harvey was assaulted by a prisoner called Bob Luke (1118-AZ). Luke knocked him unconscious and broke his jaw:

I got hit by a laundry cart. The person pushing it – Luke – wanted to be the big man on campus and told everyone he had hit me and broken my jaw. He did it with the cart, and I don't think he meant to do it. But who knows? He, and no one else.

On April 2, 1960, Harvey Carignan was paroled:

I arrived in Duluth, Minnesota, in the second week of April 1960. It was a beautiful spring, the snow had melted, and by the end of the month I had a job drawing union wages of 2.42 dollars an hour. However, I drove 90 miles each way to work, and it was too much for me, so I went and got a job under a different name on "the high bridge" which was then being built between Duluth and Superior, Wisconsin. Why under a false name? Because my federal case worker would not have signed off on the change, so I kept it secret. Several weeks later, a guy from a company called Chung King offered me a job at nine dollars an hour and I fell all over myself taking it. Not far into the job I found out he wanted me to beat the hell out of girls working there who would not let him have his way with them or were trying to get the others to strike for higher wages. I was not about to have anything to do with that, so I simply did not show up for work and was soon broke. My brother and I started pulling burglaries and that kept us in money until we happened to be driving by where someone else was pulling a burglary and got stopped. We were dressed for burglaring and had the stuff in the trunk, so we were taken to jail. I took a two-year suspended sentence for attempted burglary, and my brother got 90 days in the county jail. The suspended sentence caused my parole from Alcatraz to be revoked and I was sent to Leavenworth for four years.

During the rest of the 1960s, Harvey did time in various prisons after being convicted of rape and burglary, but in 1972 he was again a free man.

And that was when his madness escalated.

In October 1972 witnesses saw Harvey drag Leslie Brock, 19, into his silver-colored truck. Her body was found a few days later.

On May 1, 1973, Kathy Miller, 15, replied to a job advertisement that Harvey had placed in a local newspaper in Washington state. The ad was for a clerk at a gas station that Harvey had rented, but when Kathy arrived he raped and killed her. Her body was found several months later, near the city of Everett. Kathy's naked body had been wrapped in plastic, her skull full of holes from hammer blows.

On Sept. 9, 1973, he picked up a 13-year old hitchhiker, Jerri Billings. Harvey forced her to perform oral sex on him while he raped her with a hammer. He released her afterward, and the terrified girl told nothing about the ordeal until several months later.

From Sept. 8 to 14, Harvey raped and sexually abused five more young women in Minnesota. His left one of them, 19-year-old Gwen Burton, partially paralyzed from the severe abuse he inflicted. Gwen's testimony during the subsequent trial gives insight into how calculating and sadistic Harvey Carignan could be:

"He stopped to help me in the Sears parking lot because my car wouldn't start, and he invited me home with him to get some tools," she testified. "I didn't say anything and he started looking real mean, like he was mad. I was frightened, and I went with him."

During the car ride Harvey demanded sex, and when Gwen refused, he threatened her with a hammer. He took her to a deserted field in Carver County, where he parked the car. He forced her to give him oral sex on three occasions while he raped her with the hammer. At one point, she asked, "Are you going to kill me?"

Harvey smiled: "You shouldn't say such things. You could give me ideas."

Gwen testified, "He told me to sit down on the blanket. The last time I remember seeing him was when I turned around and I saw him walking behind the car with a hammer in his hand."

Harvey knocked her unconscious. When she woke up she was lying in a pool of blood. The seriously-injured girl then crawled for more than three hours before she finally found someone who could help her:

"At first I was just going to lie back down and go to sleep," she said during the trial. "Then I remembered my sister had called me that morning and said she was pregnant, and I wanted to see the baby, so I decided I'd better try to get help."

A schoolgirl named Kathy Schultz, 18, was not as lucky as Gwen Burton. On Sept. 20, Harvey picked her up in Minneapolis and offered her a ride to Washburn High School. Her badly-mangled body – she had been murdered by several hammer blows to the head

– was found the following day in a cornfield in Isanti County near the community of Dalbo, Minnesota.

With the help of witness statements from some of the rape victims, the police arrested Harvey Carignan a few days later, on Sept. 24, 1974:

"It has never could be proven, but in my opinion Harvey Carignan is the world's worst serial killer," Russell Krueger, former chief investigator for the Minneapolis police, said in the television documentary "The Want-Ad Killer" (Mainline, 1995).

Krueger – and others who have studied Carignan's crimes – think he may have committed as many as 50 murders over a large area of the United States during the early 1970s. They base this on a map that police found in Harvey Carignan's car:

"The map had 143 marks, or circles, from Ohio all the way up to Oregon, Washington, California, Vancouver," Krueger said. "We were able to confirm that there was a dead body part of a young girl in over 50 of these marked places."

Harvey Carignan was sentenced to 150 years in prison for two murders – those of Eileen Hunley and Kathy Schultz – and two counts of rape. Prosecutors chose not to pursue a trial in several other cases in which he was the prime suspect, to save time and financial resources.

I wrote back to Carignan and asked him to recount his crimes. Why did he do it? Does he think about those girls now? Does he regret it?]

The answer comes at the end of February of 2016. The next typewritten letter, number 40732, is just as friendly as the first. Harvey Carignan ends eight pages with his signature, with the Y in "Harvey" shaped like a smiley face.

But both this letter and the following ones are more pompous and intellectual in tone than the first one. Harvey spends several haphazard pages discussing Marxism, Freud, Jung, the atheist neuroscientist Sam Harris and Plato's "Republic." He tells me about his favorite book (Leo Tolstoy's "War and Peace"), his favorite movie ("Gone with the Wind"), his favorite philosopher (Immanuel Kant), his favorite poem (Wendell Berry's "The Peace of Wild Things"), and so on. It's hard to keep up with his thought processes, but after a while he gradually approaches the burning question that I want him to answer: "Why did you kill?"

Do you believe that a man is not his crimes? A man is who he is at the moment in time in which he stands. Correctionalists do not agree: it would cost them their jobs and the jobs of their children to believe such a thing. I have about me an inherent dignity that many see and understand, but not those who could help me.

```
Take care, my new-found friend. I like you. Don't give up writing
to me after you have the material for your book. I think we
could find a lot to share and to write about.

May the force be with you.


Harvey
```

I'm a horrible man because I killed human beings. Navy Seals are good men, heroes, because they killed certain Muslims: they had a compelling reason. Who says I did not, and who has the right to assume that the conviction will be with me forever? Life is a screwed up situation for each of us, but more so for me than others it would appear.

Have I made peace with myself? What is peace? Surely it is not self-satisfaction, which I have not found. Do I like and trust who I am? Absolutely! Why am I not out? Write and ask the King County prosecutor in Seattle, Washington. Who knows? It might even be my fault!!!!

His letter leads to more questions than answers. He writes about being an atheist, so why did he claim to be following "God's orders" when he committed murders? And can he seriously compare the bestial murders of innocent young women to soldiers killing in battle?

I want to know more about his background, his parents and the role they played in shaping him. But I tread lightly when I ask my questions in the following letters, realizing that a morally indignant tone would lead nowhere and could cause him to become angry and cut me off.

What is the worst thing about incarceration, you asked. The answer is "I do not know," but I mostly feel that it is the lost ability to do things and to go places when I feel like one or the other. Yes, there are limits elsewhere and they may be even more demanding of us than those in prison because there are more things in the free society to do than in prison and we would be curtailed in our wishes and hopes much more often.

Harvey Carignan, 2016

Is it a sea breeze that I miss? No, I think not; after all, I was ten years on Alcatraz and there were sea breezes there that I never think of, let alone miss. A full moon on a cloudless night? No, I saw one just this summer while in the courtyard. It was different, but I had seen them when I was young and lived on the prairies of North Dakota. The air is most clear there, and I think the moon may be more visible there than on any place on earth.

Yes, I did have a religious phase and you may have read somewhere that I said my crimes were inspired by God. But that was long after I gave up the belief in a God. It was not my idea, nor my attorney's, it was a policeman who pretended he wanted to help me so I might serve some time but not serve all of my life in prison. As it is, he fixed it so that I am spending the total of my life in prison. Oh well, I had served sentences before, and I should have known better than to believe a policeman. They never are on the side of crime or the criminals!

I had a good stepfather, but my mother instilled in me that I would not trust him. Long, long afterwards I learned that I did trust him, but had not let it show, and I resented my mother for that evermore. My stepfather was a good man, and deserving of the knowledge that I liked, even loved, and trusted him. He died shortly after I told him when I was past forty-five years old and realized it would have been ever so much better if I had told him and proved it as a child rather than telling him as an adult. Oh, well, I hope you understand. This is not easy to express, and much more to a stranger who knew neither of us then nor what life was like for us and between us way back in my childhood.

I had no relationship with my father, unless he was the "uncle" my mother used to send me to Montana to visit during several summer months of more than one year. I have had strangers tell me that he, indeed, was my father and I have had others tell me that he died in a car crash in 1929 or 1930. Still others have appraised me that he was a doctor who practiced law in Missouri until he was 111 years of age.

Please, it was facetiously that I mentioned the SEALS killing terrorists and my having committed murders in the same breath! I am well aware of the difference. The two women I killed did pose threats to me, but not to my life, to my livelihood. Do I regret what I did? Of course, absolutely, and, yes, I felt justified at the time, but not now for a very long time.

Most who have studied Harvey Carignan's crimes believe that he is guilty of far more than the two murders he was finally convicted of in 1975. But it is of course understandable that he does not volunteer having committed any more murders in our correspondence. After all, he still harbors a faint hope that he will be released before he dies:

I cannot explain what it was, but after reading "Crime and Punishment" by Fyodor Dostoyevsky, my past dissipated and scattered to the winds. I found a new direction, the one I am heading at this time. My mind allowed me to wander freely, whether I am in prison or not. This in spite of the fact I am not free and probably never will be other than in my mind.

The last time I appeared before the parole board, I was ready to leap into the free society as a good and responsible citizen. I did not make parole, but I am in that crouch. Please, believe me.

Harvey obviously never forgave his mother for destroying his relationship with his stepfather. He claims that he was about 45 years old when his stepfather died, which would have been in 1971 or 1972 – exactly the same time that he went on his killing spree. The correlation seems so obvious that I am surprised he doesn't mention it in the letter. Or am I simplifying his motive? Is it really possible that the grief he felt over losing a father figure could lead to so much evil and hate?

The answer is no, at least according to Carignan himself:

Please, do not draw a line between my crimes and the anger you believe I must have felt for women. The one has nothing to do with the other. More than anything, anabolic steroids and my own stupidity are to blame for most of what I did wrong. I always saw my mother for what she was: a struggling soul who wanted better than she had, and had no one to blame except her children, and me in particular, for not attaining those goals. Her dream was to marry a professional man and become someone other than what she was: the wife of a poor farmer and day laborer. Any anger in my record directed toward her was put there by well-meaning and not so well-meaning psychiatrists who could not find the answers because I would not give them to them and they fell back on the old bugaboo: it was his mother's fault.

Did I like her? Hell no, I did not like her. Did I blame her? Not in the least. She was a victim of her circumstances, just as I became one of mine.

Why I was happy to be able to tell my stepfather on his deathbed that I had loved him and still loved him was because it made him so happy. I had not seen him in years, and my mother had turned all of her other children against him when, in fact, it was her fault that he had divorced her, she had given birth to a black baby. No one in the family knew it except she and I myself did not find out until a black half-nephew wrote to me from Chicago.

Murder, to my way of thinking, is seldom a willful action so far as the mental process is concerned although it must be so far as the physical process is an integral part of it. I like to think of myself as someone who suffered greatly due to a lack of an ability for dialogue and being unable to explain his mind or actions since a very early age.

There is a saying that "without empathy, conscience and remorse, one can commit murder." I am here to tell you that with these qualities one can commit murder.

***

Eileen Marie Hunley was born July 17, 1945. In her book "The Want-Ad Killer" Ann Rule describes her as a friendly, deeply religious member of the Jehovah's Witnesses.

On a cold Minnesota night in January 1974, a big, burly man assisted Eileen and two of her girlfriends when their car broke down. The man's name was Harvey Carignan, and he offered them a ride home. They willingly agreed, and Eileen's friends would later remember Harvey as helpful and "charming." Harvey took a fancy to Eileen, and he called her a few weeks later. He presented himself as a faithful Catholic, and although Eileen Hunley was a "witness," she apparently took comfort in him at least being a Christian. Ann Rule also describes her as being attracted to the idea of providing spiritual "guidance" to him, and she started dating the almost 20-years-older Harvey in the spring of 1974. The relationship quickly became serious. In June, they even paid a visit to Eileen's parents in her hometown of Goessel, Kansas.

But in July the relationship began to fall apart, partly because Carignan got drunk on several occasions and frightened Eileen with sudden fits of rage. She broke up with him, but said she hoped they could "remain friends."

Saturday, Aug. 10, 1974, was a hot, sultry day in Minneapolis. It was also the last day anyone saw Eileen Hunley alive. The next day she didn't show up for church, and when she didn't report to her job as a preschool teacher the following Monday, her worried friends alerted the police. Officers found her apartment untouched.

Her criminal ex-boyfriend Harvey soon came under suspicion, but he couldn't be tied to her disappearance.

Have you ever met the love of your life? I ask him in a letter.

"I have given great thought to your question," Carignan answers two weeks later.

"Yes, I did, and I am serving a life sentence of first degree murder

at the present time because I killed her."
It's obvious that he's talking about Eileen Hunley. Her corpse was
found dumped in a field in Shelbourne County, Minnesota, more
than a month after her disappearance in 1974. A tree branch had
been placed in her vagina. Carignan's version of how he killed her is
both complex and unlikely:

*Believe me, I didn't want to but I did it while in the process of getting her off
my back while fighting another person.*

*[...] I had taken a trip to Ohio, and Eileen was supposed to have gone with
me. However, when it was time to go, I could not find her. I thought she may have
taken a trip to Kansas, which she sometimes did, even taking my car and not
telling me she was going. When I came back from Ohio, I went to the house,
opened the door and let myself in. It was then I noticed that the screen on the side
kitchen window was pushed in. We had lots of money in the headboard of the bed,
and when I checked, it was all gone.*

*I sat down to ponder about that which I had seen and I heard Eileen's voice
coming in through the back door that I had left open. I looked out and saw her
nowhere, but I saw a van and there was a guy I knew by having seen him before,
so I walked down there and asked, "Have you seen Eileen?" He answered: "Get
out of here, punk, or I'll kick your ass all over the place." Well, I had begun to
use anabolic steroids as soon as I left Alcatraz and was as big as a horse and
about twice as strong. I pulled him out of the window by his head and kicked the
living hell out of him. Then I went to the back of the van and opened the side door
on the other side, and Eileen was there with a black dude I had seen before but
did not know. She was only wearing a tee shirt and a pair of argyle socks; the rest
of her clothes were neatly folded over her arm.*

*She said "Harvey, these guys raped me!" I told her, "put on your clothes and
go into the house and I'll take care of this." At that time the guy on the ground
rolled over and bit me in the leg. I began to stomp him, and Eileen jumped on my
back telling me that it was not him but the black dude who had raped her. I was
angry as hell. The black guy ran away. I turned around and threw Eileen off my
back over my shoulder and stomped her as I had the guy who was lying there
beside her.*

Cars were passing by, but none of them stopped and it appears that none of them called the police. I looked at the mess the two people on the ground were, and got enough of my mind back to begin trying to help Eileen. What happened to the other guy I do not know, and I do not care. Eileen had dropped her clothing on the ground, so I picked them up, put them on my car seat, and put her in the car on top of them and began to drive to Memorial Hospital. All I could think of was to get Eileen to the hospital and to get her help.

Right on the main drag of Minneapolis, Hennepin Avenue, across the street from a bar where I used to get my checks cashed, she turned stiff and urinated and defecated on her clothes. I knew she was dead, so I stopped the car and went to the trunk and got a U-Haul blanket. I wrapped her in the blanket and put her in the trunk. I saw a man standing there watching what I was doing and he asked: "What do you think you're doing?" I told him to get the hell away from me and threw Eileen's dirty clothes at him and hit him in the face with them. He looked at me like he had discovered the way to the moon or something, and said: "Man, that is shit!"

I drove away, wanting to take Eileen to a funeral parlor, but I did not know anyone who owned one in Minneapolis so I drove a hundred and fifty miles to the city of Duluth. I stayed the night at a friend's home, and the next morning I went to the car and opened the door. The stench almost knocked me on my back. I hurried to the funeral parlor that I knew, but it was closed. I took off for Minneapolis again, and was going to take her to one near where I lived. Not tell the people, just bring her in the back and leave a bunch of money for them.

When I got as far as a little town called Milaca I saw a hog pen, and I stopped and put Eileen in it, blanket and all. After driving awhile, I changed my mind and drove back. When I got there, there was a man loading her in either a 1968 or 1969 red Ford pick-up, and he drove away like a bat out of hell. I followed him from quite a distance behind. He ended up going into a side road. He lifted her out and across a fence, crawled over himself and took her into the woods. When he came back, he drove away, probably more scared than I had been when I put her in the trunk on Hennepin Avenue.

When I was getting ready to go into the woods to see if I could find Eileen an old man came out and carried her to the fence, put her over, and stepped into a corn patch where the plants were not so tall. He took the blanket off her, examined her orifices, probably looking for valuables, rolled up the blanket, put it under his arm, and left. Just when I was going to get Eileen a police car appeared. I said to myself: "Hell, that's not Eileen any longer, only her body." I was somewhat religious at the time and thought her soul had left her. I decided she was dead, and there was nothing I could do for her any longer, so I drove off. When they found her 40 days later she again had been moved.

When I finish reading Harvey's story, I sit staring at the letterhead for a long time. I do not believe his vulgar, scattershot story for a moment, but – paradoxically – I still have a feeling that this letter is the most "true" of the ones he has sent me. It's finally the real Carignan – liar, misogynist, sexual deviant, cold-blooded murderer. Everything else we've talked about – the intellectual discussions of philosophy, poetry and literature, the friendly well-wishes, the happy smileys – suddenly feels like a thin veneer over a soul that is deeply decayed.

***

In a prison in Faribault, Minnesota, Harvey Carignan lives on and on – 69 years after he committed his first murder. As he writes in one of his letters to me:

"Whoever thought I would live to be ninety and may go on to be one-hundred?"

Despite his age, every now and then he reveals a hot temper. When I become too intrusive in my questioning regarding his fight with Bob Luke at Alcatraz, he gets angry and tells me to "go to hell." In late 2016, he tells me about a fight he recently had with a fellow inmate:

About two months ago I slapped a big-mouthed idiot in the mouth and did not get caught, but someone seemed to believe I should have and sent an unsigned "kite" to the unit lieutenant which caused her to check the cameras and I got five days in segregation. My property was taken and when I returned much of it was missing.

He is a strange mix of a crotchety old man and a calculating liar – probably a textbook example of a psychopath. In one of the letters, Harvey at least seems to realize that he, if anyone, should be lying cold and dead in the ground – and not Eileen Hunley or any other of his murder victims:

I still love and miss her, and I'm most dreadfully sorry for her part much more than for mine. She did not deserve to die and no one other than nature decrees when it is time.

1118-AZ

Some people manage to turn the page. Others don't.

Some people drive around in the same destructive and hopeless ruts throughout their lives; others succeed in reinventing themselves, shedding their skins, and moving on.

The journey out of darkness is seldom as long and dramatic as it was for Bob Luke, and not just figuratively speaking. In 1954, he sat naked and hungry in a cold and pitch-black cell on Alcatraz, without any hope for the future. But many years later, he found hope and light, in the form of a woman who loved him, despite all his shortcomings.

Bob dared to turn the page.

On the other side was happiness.

***

Two snapshots from Bob Luke's life:

It's a summer night in 1954, and Alcatraz is enveloped in darkness. The island's lighthouse casts its beams onto San Francisco Bay, and behind the thick walls of the cell house, roughly 300 of America's most dangerous men are soundly asleep. But at four o'clock in the morning, the calm is shattered.

Prisoner 1118-AZ in cell block C has had enough of his cramped cell. His name is Robert "Bob" Luke, 27, and he has only been in for three months. But the realization that he will be stuck here for years to come – trapped in a space of only 9 by 5 feet– sends him into a rage. He starts screaming.

"I tried to set my mattress on fire, and I threw out all my possessions. Then I put some stuff in the toilet so it started flooding, and water began to flow out in the cell house," Bob remembers many years later.

Guards rush to pull him away to cell block D. There, waiting for him, is "the Hole" – the dark cell that all prisoners at Alcatraz fear:

"They forced me to strip naked. Then they closed the thick cell door, and everything went black. You couldn't see anything. There was no bed, no furniture, nothing. Not even a blanket. I began to freeze almost immediately," Bob says.

"And there I remained, for 29 days."

***

The second snapshot comes many years later, in the 1970s. Bob Luke is approaching 50 and lives in northern California, where he is working as a docker. He has a failed marriage behind him, and a son. Life on the outside has been difficult, but he has managed to stay free since 1959, the year of his release from Alcatraz.

Now he is on a date with a young woman named Ida. Bob has fallen in love with her, but there's a problem: He's been holding something

33

back, and now he feels compelled to tell her about his darkest secret.

"He didn't tell me on our first date that he had been on Alcatraz. But he told me on our second one," Ida says, smiling.

Were you shocked? I ask.

"No. His personality was so wonderful. He was so well educated and had such a good vocabulary. And he treated me like a princess," she replies.

The date went well. Today, Bob and Ida have been married for more than 40 years.

***

His voice is weak, he moves with the aid of a walker, and he has a nasal cannula to help him breathe. But Bob Luke's eyes are as sparkling blue as they were in the 1950s, when his icy stare while robbing backs earned him the nickname "Cold Blue".

We meet on Fisherman's Wharf in San Francisco's harbor, on a windy day in May 2015. Bob, now 88, has just taken the ferry back to the city after spending the day out on Alcatraz signing his book, "Entombed in Alcatraz", for wide-eyed tourists. The ferry ride takes only ten minutes, but from 1954 to 1959 it was a trip he could only make in his dreams.

"I could never have imagined that Alcatraz would become a museum one day, or that people would look at me like some kind of rock star," he says, shaking his head.

Ida Luke is a friendly, short statured woman with alert, peering eyes, and she doesn't leave Bob's side for a second during our interview.

"Isn't Bob's book amazing?" she says to me with hopeful eyes.

"He really has a talent for writing. And it's apparent that he read many books when he was in prison!"

***

Robert Victor Luke was born on May 22, 1927 and grew up in a large family that moved around from Utah to Wyoming to California. As a teenager, he started committing petty thefts that escalated to burglary, and finally to bank robbery. He was arrested for robbing a bank in Los Angeles in 1952 and was sentenced to ten years in prison.

"I started getting into trouble when I was 16. Then I went straight for a while and enlisted in the Navy. But I had a terrible temper when I was young, and I always ended up in fights. My problem was that I could do time. Being locked up didn't bother me," he says.

In the early 1950s Bob Luke shuffled from prison to prison. In early 1954 he tried to escape from Leavenworth in Kansas, and thus stamped his ticket to Alcatraz, where he arrived three months later:

"I can still remember the first day I came out here with the boat. Everyone who came here had, of course, heard of Alcatraz. But I had heard mostly good stuff: everybody had their own cell which was important, the food was good, you had the yard on weekends and work was mandatory. Plus, they had a great library! What more could you ask for? So there was nothing to be afraid of," he says with a wry smile.

"All that was true. But you sat for 15 hours a day in the same cell and were forced to do exactly what the guards said. Same thing, same day, at the same time. You couldn't wander freely anywhere."

There was also the risk of witnessing – or being subjected to – severe violence:

"People beat each other up all the time. I saw people being stabbed, some died. But I was never afraid for my own safety, because I was good at fighting. If someone said something I didn't like I would just walk up and punch them in the face."

One person he didn't like was Harvey Carignan. In his book, Bob describes how he worked in the laundry alongside Carignan, who he describes as lazy and annoying:

"He wanted to be part of our group, but he came on too quick, and we didn't trust him. We also knew that he had a 'shiv' stashed somewhere in the laundry and always had it on his person. He was also a convicted killer. One day when I had had enough of Carrignan's [sic] crap, and no longer caring about the consequences, I went looking for him. […] Knowing he had a 'shiv', I simply walked up to him and hit him with my fists four or five times. He went down unconscious and I turned and went back to work on the dryers. Someone called the guards and he told them he had slipped and fallen down. Except his jaw was shattered, and so were his cheekbones."

Harvey Carignan confirms that Bob Luke broke his jaw, but according to him, Bob pushed a heavy laundry cart at him and then lied to the other prisoners about what had really happened. When I –

via email, long after our initial meeting in San Francisco – asked Bob to comment on this, he became annoyed:

"I am not going to get into a shouting match with a rapist, serial killer and pathological liar", he wrote back to me. "Every interview he has done is different. My account in my book stands."

***

One of the dark cells in cellblock D

The prisoners were given different jobs on the island. Bob Luke first worked in the kitchen, which he didn't like. That was partly why he exploded in his cell one night, which led to an extended stay in the "Hole"– and nearly a month of cold, darkness and hunger:

"Everything is made of steel around you, it was dark and cold and I had no clothes. The toilet was a hole in the ground. I got bread and water once a day, and every third day, I got some food. It was tough. The only time I saw daylight was when they opened the door to give me the food," he says.

"But you got used to it. I did pushups and walked around in the cell to keep me warm. Then I slept a little, until I woke up from the cold. Then I started to move around again," he continues.

It sounds like torture, I tell him. But Bob waves his hand dismissively:

"You get used to it."

A few days before our meeting, I interviewed a former guard at Alcatraz, George DeVincenzi, and he questioned Bob Luke's assertion that he had spent 29 days in the Hole:

"That would have been illegal. A prisoner could sit there for a maximum of 19 days at a time. I think Bob has got the numbers 19 and 29 mixed up," DeVincenzi said.

Bob and Ida Luke, San Francisco, 2015

Bob Luke is an old and weak man now, but when I tell him what the former guard said he gets angry, and I catch a glimpse of the bad-tempered bank robber he once was:

"Oh, that's bullshit! The guards did what they wanted to us! It was the warden who decided the rules. If you asked him, he would say that 19 days was the maximum, but I know a guy who sat there for 90 days," he says indignantly.

We are in a café in the harbor, and Bob's mood suddenly turns sour:

"Does anybody smoke in here?" he says, and stares at a few terrified teenagers who frantically shake their heads.

"No? I can smell smoke!"

"No, Bob, there's no smoke," Ida says. After a while, Bob calms down.

***

After his release from the Hole, Bob Luke kept a low profile on the island. In the years that followed, he focused on doing his time as quietly as possible.

"You shut off your emotions. That's the only way to cope," he says.

For more than a year, Bob celled next door to one of the prison's most notorious inmates. Alvin "Creepy" Karpis (325-AZ) was one of the few remnants from the notorious gangster era of the 1930s, when FBI Director J. Edgar Hoover put a "Most Wanted" label on America's worst criminals. But Bob says he never talked to Karpis. Not even a hello, even though they slept just a few feet apart, seven days a week, 365 days a year.

That's a bit weird, I say.

"No, it's not weird," Bob says.

"I only talked to four or five other prisoners, people that I knew. The less you talked to people, the less likely you were to get in trouble."

Perhaps that is why Bob has relatively few clear memories of his time on Alcatraz. His mind has compressed five years to a handful of random events, perhaps as a coping mechanism. The rest, he has forgotten; Bob has, for example, no memory of the two escape attempts made during his time on the island.

But one of his memories is crystal clear. One day – after he had spent about four years on Alcatraz – Bob sat in the yard and looked out at the Golden Gate Bridge. Then he had an epiphany that would change his life:

"The wind was blowing, and suddenly I could smell newly mown grass. I started thinking: why can't I smell grass more often? How did I end up here?" Bob says.

"Then it dawned on me that I only had myself to blame for being in prison. It was nobody's else's fault. And when I realized that, I decided to do everything in my power to become free again."

On April 26, 1959, Bob Luke was released. To ease the adjustment from life on the inside to life on the outside, Alcatraz prisoners were usually transferred first to other, less-restrictive prisons before being released outright. But Bob was one of only seven inmates in the history of Alcatraz freed directly from the prison.

On the day he was released, Bob was taken by boat to Fort Mason where a guard escorted him to a taxi. Together, they went to San Francisco International Airport, where Bob boarded a plane to Los Angeles to meet his family.

The conversion was so abrupt as to border on being inhumane. One moment he was sitting, as usual, in his little closet-sized cell. The next moment he was a free, 32-year-old man in a plane, who had his whole life ahead of him.

"I couldn't be around any type of argument, because I was very violent and had a bad temper. If I saw someone who looked like trouble I would just walk away. I also had a large family that supported me," Bob says.

"I would say that the first two years were incredibly difficult. I was completely confused. To go from such a small place, to a large place with lots of loud noises everywhere, and seeing women walking around…it was tough."

Bob Luke on April 26, 1959, the day he was released from Alcatraz

Bob Luke worked a variety of jobs, got married, had a son, divorced, got married again. Above all, he succeeded where many others described in this book failed: He managed to stay out of trouble. From 1959 on, he has been a free man. These days he and Ida are happy seniors, living north of San Francisco. Every now and then, they take the ferry over to Alcatraz where he once lived in confinement:

"In 2010, I returned to Alcatraz for the first time in over 50 years," he says.

"I was a bit apprehensive, I didn't know how people would react. But everyone has been so kind to me. For many years, I never told anyone that I had done time on Alcatraz, because I was ashamed of it. But I no longer feel that way."

The first Bob Luke did when he was released in 1959 was to visit his brother Darwin in Los Angeles.

"When I arrived at his house, I sat down on his front lawn. His family wondered what was wrong with me," Bob remembers, laughing.

"But I just had to. It was so important for me to smell grass again."

***

Author's note: The Swedish version of this book was published in September 2017. I sent a copy to Bob and Ida (knowing, of course, they wouldn't be able to understand a word of it). The book reached their northern California home on October 2. Bob was severely ill by then, and lying in bed.

"I said, enthusiastically: 'Look, Jon's book'. He said, 'read it to me', but it was in Swedish, so I told him about the photos and we had a good laugh," Ida later told me.

Bob Luke passed away later that day, October 2, 2017, at the age of 90. He was the first person who agreed to be interviewed for this book, and I owe both him and Ida a big debt of gratitude. Rest in peace, Bob.

1186-AZ

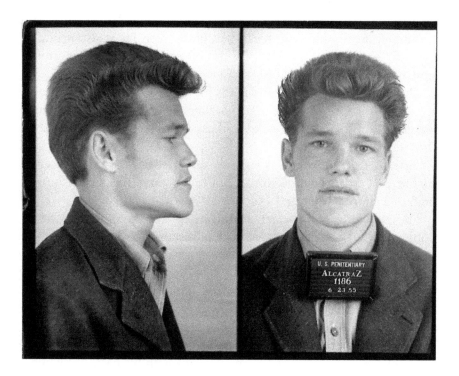

Charlie Hopkins had a knife. That knife was used to murder another prisoner in the shower room on Alcatraz. But Charlie didn't do it. The killer was his best friend – and Charlie begged him not to go through with it.

"But he was so stubborn," Charlie remembers. "Nothing I said could make him change his mind."

The line between life and death could certainly be razor thin on the island. Two friends had a falling out, that's all. Nothing extraordinary. Just another human life extinguished by violence.

***

It's the middle of the night on Alcatraz, and in a cell 25-year-old Charles "Charlie" Hopkins jerks awake in his cell when someone places something on his pillow. It's a scrap of paper that has been passed on along from cell to cell, with a message to Charlie from another prisoner.

It is July 1957. Charlie has been on the island for two years. He's one of the younger inmates and has a face fit for Hollywood – a winning smile, skin that is chronically sun-bleached from his years growing up in Florida, and thick, dark-blond hair. He is also prone to violence, shaped by a tragic childhood and years spent in tough orphanages and youth centers.

Charlie unfolds the note and reads it:

"It was a short sex note that this dingbat had sent me. He was a pervert. He told me how good-looking I was, and that he liked to have sex with other men.

"So, the next morning, as soon as they opened the cells, I waited for the guy. Then I knocked the hell out of him and kicked him in the face a couple of times."

The unfortunate prisoner had learned a lesson about Charlie Hopkins. Charlie walked around with a burning anger in his chest – a rage that stood in contrast to his otherwise friendly, slightly shy demeanor.

I call him one evening in late 2016. Charlie is a retiree living in the small community of Green Cove Springs, Florida, just outside the city of Jacksonville, where he was born March 17, 1932.

He has remained law-abiding since the 1960s. He seems friendly, and I get the impression he has made peace with his past. But when I ask him about his childhood, he becomes quiet.

"I had a bad childhood," he says after a while.

"But I have written a few pages about it. I can send them to you."

***

Charlie tells me that he has penned an autobiography that has never been published, and he gives me permission to quote sections of it.

A few weeks after our conversation, I receive a thick letter in the mail. I start reading his typewritten manuscript – a straightforward, unsentimental portrayal of a tough life, the story of a boy born into a world with odds stacked heavily against him.

The earliest I can remember is when I was about five years old. The year was 1937 and I can still see my mother, Dessie, and foster father John, riding in the front seat of an old jalopy along the roads between Florida and Tennessee. Back and forth we would go, mom, dad, me, my three stepbrothers, and my stepsister, looking for any kind of work to make a little money.

At night our family would camp on the side of some dirt road near a little stream, if we could find one, and cook by a campfire. We kids would fight as all kids do or play the best way we could. My stepbrothers were Carl, Mule and Elmo. I was closest to my stepsister, Margaret. Just like so many other Depression-era families, we had no good clothes or shoes to speak of and we surely never had enough to eat. Even though we were always hungry, my stepfather was too proud to ask farmers nearby for food. My mother, who had conceived me when she was fourteen by some guy passing through and had married John at fifteen, told me years later that my stepfather was too religious and kind to make it in a system like ours.

John Hopkins was 32 when he took me and my mother on. Carl, Mule, Elmo and Margaret were born soon after. John always wanted to do the right thing and depended on God to take care of the rest. John was so gentle in spirit that he allowed another man to take my mother away from him. And because that poor excuse of a wife-grabber didn't want us kids, she just left without us. She then had four more children, all by the newcomer. But six years later my mother gave all those kids away, too, when another man came along and asked her to go away with him.

But John at least had the courage to try and make it in society with the five of us and no wife. One of the haunting memories I carry occurred shortly after my mother deserted us. My friend Bobby, my first boyhood friend, was abandoned along with his brothers and sisters by his mother too. His father was so poor he had to beg from door to door in west Jacksonville, Florida, to feed his five children. One night he returned home empty handed. Because his kids were starving and crying, he shot them all and then shot himself. I think about Bobby all the time and the life he never had because his father could get no job or food. John at least wouldn't quit. Bobby's father did. From that time on, I decided that I would never, never, never give up, no matter what.

To this day, I don't hate my mother for what she did. She was a child when she brought me into the world and probably did the best she could with what little she had. At least she wasn't like some unfortunate girls in those days who in order to feed their children left them in the front seat of their broken-down car while they prostituted themselves in the back seat. I know pathetic women like that are too weak to last long in our society.

Like most delinquents, I started stealing very early. I was in the first grade at Central Riverside Elementary School in Jacksonville and I can still hear our teacher, Miss York, announce to the class, "We have a thief in this room and I mean to find out who it is and punish him." I was scared silly because I was the thief. I took lunch money off the kids desks when everyone was at recess. [...] I was a compulsive thief and felt no remorse about it whatsoever. I needed money desperately and some of the kids had it.

Soon, I was stealing bicycles and shoplifting four or five comic books a day. I loved comic books and my favorites were Captain Marvel, Supersnipe, Batman, Dick Tracy, Boy Commandos, Blackhawk, and my most favorite of all, Crime Does Not Pay. Through Crime Does Not Pay comics I became acquainted with Alvin "Creepy" Karpis. Years later when I met him at Alcatraz I told him it seemed I had known him all my life. A prison psychiatrist told me that all I was stealing in my childhood years was love – that I was trying to fill myself up with the love and caring my mother wasn't giving me. Maybe he was right.

In his teens, Charlie's shoplifting and petty stealing landed him in various foster homes and juvenile delinquency centers. He also started boxing, and he proved to have a talent for it. In the early 1950s he was sentenced to a short prison term for burglary, which he served in the state prison in Raiford, Florida.

"When I was released in 1952, a real bad guy that I had met in prison looked me up," Charlie tells me on the phone. "I lived in Miami at the time. His name was James Francis Hill, and we got together. He wanted to free a friend of his that worked on the chain gang in Florida. Then we started doing some robberies together."

The two men became increasingly careless. On one occasion, they robbed and kidnapped an elderly couple, but the couple escaped when Charlie and his partner stopped at a red light in Tennessee. Hopkins and Hill evaded authorities by hiding in a forest, while police planes circled overhead, but they were soon caught.

"I was sentenced to 17 years," Charlie tells me. "At first, I got sent to Atlanta, but I always ended up in trouble there. At the beginning of '55 I beat up a couple of guys, and that's when they sent me to the Rock."

He was 23 when he arrived on the island in February 1955. Charlie became prisoner 1186-AZ.

***

Alcatraz was to be his home for three years. Still, as an old man, Charlie remembers small, seemingly insignificant details from day-to-day life behind the thick walls of the prison.

I have in my mind snapshots: endless glances up and down Broadway[2]; inmates sweeping and humming; inmates carrying towels, squeegees, and buckets; endless cleaning, scrubbing, polishing, scraping, and painting; guards with clipboards; loud buzzers: the opening, closing, banging, and clicking of doors; the flushing of toilets; the library and hospital being opened each day; the dining room and kitchen being cleaned up after meals; laundry being collected from cell to cell; inmates being searched on their way out to the recreation yard; shouting throughout the cell house; loud singing, and the playing of small musical instruments; the close-ups of those I liked and hated: the dinner trays being passed to those in isolation or solitary confinement; the buzzing motors in the industries; to say nothing of the other endless routine prison duties.

Despite his youth, Charlie – or "Hoppy," as the other prisoners called him – quickly earned the respect of the older inmates at Alcatraz. For a short while he worked as a gardener – one of the island's most coveted jobs, because you got to spend time out in the open air.

But Charlie soon earned a reputation for being something of a

---

[2] A nickname for the corridor between cell blocks B and C.

problem prisoner. This led to him spending time in the dark isolation cells of cell block D, on multiple occasions.

"I was in and out of the Hole all the time. Sometimes for fighting, or talking back to guards … And I was also involved in an escape plot," he tells me over the phone.

"A few guys – Teddy Green (1180-AZ), Larry Trumblay (1129-AZ) and Forrest Tucker (1047-AZ) – had an escape plot going. I wasn't going with them, but I helped them get some tools. I got a hacksaw from a guy named 'Red' Winhoven (772-AZ) that he stole from the machine shop."

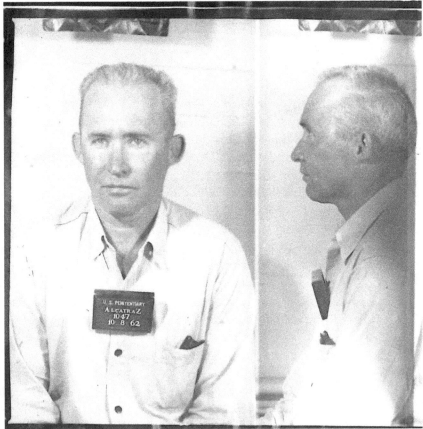

Forrest Tucker, 1047-AZ

The three men planned to cut through the bars of a basement window under the kitchen, then slip down to the water. According to Charlie, the plan was well underway in the waning days of the winter of 1957.

"They had cut through the bars and used black shoe polish and soap to cover the tracks. But they got busted before they could carry out the escape," he says.

"The guards found their tools. They had made holes in the toilet bowls in their cells, and then hid the stuff there."

Charlie had a similar hole – although it was empty – in his own toilet bowl. He appeared before the Disciplinary Board on March 13, 1957, with several guards and the deputy warden, J. B. Latimer, interrogating him.

A transcript of the hearing – which Charlie sent to me – shows him professing his innocence.

Hopkins: I don't know anything.

Mr. Latimer: We have been watching you for some time, Hopkins. You have been quite a busybody, running packages between Trumblay, Green and the other inmates.

Hopkins: I don't know any more about them than anybody else. They're just like anybody else to me.

Mr. Latimer: My actual belief is that you are a runner. Maybe you weren't in on the actual plan.

Hopkins: I don't know anything about it at all.

The Disciplinary Board was not impressed by Charlie's attempt to feign unawareness of the escape plan. The panel added ten days of to his sentence. He also had to spend several months locked up in isolation in cell block D, along with the three would-be escapees.

Because the plot was averted so quickly, it's seldom included in the 14 fourteen "official" escape attempts that were made in the history of Alcatraz. But it did pave the way for the island's final bona fide escape attempt – in December 1962, more than five years later – when prisoners John Paul Scott (1403-AZ) and Darryl Lee Parker (1413-AZ) made their way down to the water.

"They went through the exact same window," Charlie says. "The prison claimed that Parker and Scott cut the bars, but it was done years before by Green and Tucker."

***

During his last year on the island, Charlie became embroiled in a tragic, bloody drama, an event that that still haunts him 60 years later. The protagonists of this drama were two prisoners – Roland Simcox (1131-AZ) and Edward Gauvin (1134-AZ) – who both arrived on Alcatraz in the summer of 1954. The two were inseparable, both serving 40-year sentences for having deserted from the military together. Alvin Karpis (325-AZ) described the two men in his book "On the Rock," published in 1979.

Simcox is by far the more aggressive of the pair. [...] He is vain. Whenever he walks on the yard he can't keep his eyes off his own chest and biceps. His t-shirt is usually rolled up over his shoulders to reveal his muscular arms. [...] Gauvin is not as strong or muscular as Simcox although he stands as tall. [...] He has as much hair as many women and this along with his feminine features give him a "chorus boy" look. He is younger than Simcox, has even white teeth, delicate lips and nose, and (although he doesn't act like an outright homosexual) it is assumed by many that he and Simcox are lovers. I know the first time I see Gauvin's innocent face in front of my cell that he will end up getting in a lot of trouble in Alcatraz or getting a lot of other people in trouble.

Charlie, who knew both Simcox and Gauvin well, disputes Karpis' description of them:

"They were in the Army together, so they were close, but I don't think they were a couple. I know people thought that, but they didn't know them, so they can't really have an opinion," Charlie tells me.

"Gauvin got sent to D-block for stabbing a guy. While he was in there, he spat in Simcox's face through the bars one time. That's why Simcox wanted to kill him.

"I tried to talk him out of it several times, but he told me, 'I've tried to forget about it, but I can't. Every time I start to think about it I start to burn, like I have a burning rage in my stomach. If you don't want to talk with me, I understand, 'cause I know you like the guy. But I have to do this."

According to Charlie, a prisoner named Willard "Red" Winhoven (772-AZ) worked in the machine shop and made crude knives for prisoners in need of them. The inmates had to pass through metal detectors when they reentered the cell house, but the knife Winhoven gave Charlie was made of a copper alloy that didn't set off any alarms.

Roland Simcox, 1131-AZ

"It was made of solid brass. That's how he got it through the 'snitch box.' It was about ten inches wide and a quarter-inch thick. I agreed to give it to Simcox, but I begged him not to go through with it."

He wrestled with conflicting emotions. On one hand, he liked Gauvin. Simcox, however, was one of Charlie's best friends.

"Gauvin wasn't a real friend of mine, just someone I knew and liked. Simcox was a friend I could depend on."

But that brings up a riddle: What exactly did Charlie like so much about Simcox, who was by all accounts one of the most ruthless, violent inmates ever to land on Alcatraz?

A few months before the conflict with Edward Gauvin, Simcox

stabbed prisoner Floyd "Dog" Mann (941-AZ) in the exercise yard. Mann narrowly survived the attack, and Simcox was later acquitted of attempted murder charges after other inmates falsely testified that he acted in self-defense.

Simcox may have been deeply deranged, which seemed even more evident after Charlie tells me about his friend's background in a letter.

"He was a combat veteran of the Korean War," Charlie writes. "And I don't know if I should tell you this, but it will show either what war does to some people, or what kind of psychopath Simcox was.

"He said he came into a village after heavy attack and had sex on a dead woman. When I busted out laughing, he said, 'What's wrong with that, man? The body was still warm!'"

An admission of necrophilia ought to have been a red flag, but Charlie explains why he still valued his friendship with Simcox.

"He may have been a dangerous psychopath, but he was loyal to his friends, and that's more than can be said for most people when the chips are down. That's why I say that the best friends I ever had were left behind on Alcatraz."

Throughout 1956 and for the first half of 1957, Edward Gauvin was locked up in cell block D for stabbing a prisoner named Joseph "San Quentin Smitty" Smith (995-AZ). Simcox couldn't get to him.

On the morning of June 6, 1957, Gauvin found out he was being transferred back into the general population. Charlie was in cell block D himself at the time for his role in the failed escape.

From his unpublished manuscript:

Gauvin came by my cell to say goodbye. I told him not to go out into the yard because he wouldn't live long. I said that I liked him and Simcox both, and that Simcox had already told me he hoped they would transfer Gauvin out of Alcatraz so he could avoid killing him. But Gauvin smiled and said, "Well, we will see what happens. I appreciate your concern, Hoppy."

He was gone about an hour and a half, when the D-block guard named Robinson shouted, "They're bringing in Simcox! He just stabbed Gauvin to death! He stabbed him in the shower room and split his heart wide open!"

Edward Gauvin, 1134-AZ

My heart sank. In all my life I hadn't felt as low as I did that moment. In fact, the whole institution felt bad about it, even the guards because they liked Gauvin too ... Simcox later told me that when he saw Gauvin coming down the steps to the shower room, he went back and got his knife out of hiding, and hid it under his belt ... Later, while Gauvin was taking a shower on the end next to the wicker wire, Simcox lit a cigarette, walked over to him, handed him the cigarette, and started talking. Three basement guards were present in the shower room since they expected trouble. One walked up and said, "All right, Simcox, move on." Simcox said, "It's OK," and kept talking to Gauvin as Gauvin dried off and put on his shorts. Then suddenly Simcox pulled his knife and began stabbing Gauvin through the heart. It happened in a flash. When Simcox saw that Gauvin was finished he walked away. But Gauvin got up, and an inmate named Lewis put his hands on Gauvin's shoulders and asked, "Are you OK, kid?" and Gauvin whispered, "Hell no, I'm not OK," and then fell to the floor.

Simcox told me that as he walked up the steps, he looked back and saw that Gauvin was bent over on his knees looking up at him with hate in his eyes.

Several guards rushed to Gauvin's aid, but claimed afterwards that the attack had happened too fast for them to save him.

"We tried to help Gauvin, but he died almost right away," former guard George DeVincenzi told me when I met him on Alcatraz. "One of the guards started throwing rolls of toilet paper at Simcox when it happened," Charlie tells me, with sadness in his voice. "Simcox was 6' 3" and built like one of these Mr. Americas. They couldn't have done anything to prevent it."

Edward Gauvin was only 23 when he died. Simcox was acquitted of his murder, after a group of inmates testified – apparently falsely – that Gauvin instigated the fight that killed him. It was part of the so-called "prison code" to always stand stick up for a fellow prisoner in trouble – even if hat prisoner had committed a brutal murder.

Roland Simcox was later released from prison, and died in 2006 at age 74. Charlie's role as the man who handed Simcox the murder weapon never came out at trial. Decades later, when I spoke to him, Charlie said he still regrets the role he played in Gauvin's death.

He puts it this way in his manuscript:

To this moment I'm ashamed. It is probably the worst thing I have ever done and I can't describe the extent I'm sorry for what I did.

***

Charlie was transferred out of Alcatraz in February of 1958. Five years later he got out of prison for good.

"I was released in 1963, but it was tough to find a job for an ex-prisoner like me," he said. "The jobs you got were bad and didn't pay any money. It took until 1967 before I got a good job carpeting at a place called Carpet City. I did that for a long time."

He remains in touch with one fellow Alcatraz ex-inmate, even though the two didn't serve time together. James "Whitey" Bulger (1428-AZ) went on a far different trajectory than Charlie after prison. While Charlie was carpeting and becoming a father, Bulger built a powerful criminal empire in Boston and soon became one of America's most notorious mafia leaders. Johnny Depp played Bulger in the film "Black Mass," portraying him as a homicidal psychopath.

"Whitey has told me several times that he is glad that I managed to stay away from trouble after prison," Charlie says. "I know that he also tried to get a job and go straight in the beginning, but he didn't find any jobs that paid enough."

Charlie is proud of his own life since prison.

"I've had it really good. I have a daughter, and she has a son. So I have a grandson. He just turned 13."

It has been almost 60 years since he boarded a boat on the Alcatraz docks, shedding his identity as prisoner 1186-AZ. But time can be elastic in the human mind. Memories of the distant past s have a way of reemerging, as if they're happening all over again.

That, at least, seems to be the case with Charles Edward Hopkins:

A day doesn't go by today that some fragment of Alcatraz life doesn't surface either in a dream or when I'm wide awake. [...] How will I ever erase from my memory the Frisco waterfront; the two great bridges; the orange ball of the sun coming up over the East Bay hills; morning and evening lights of commuters on the bridges; the white sailing boats and fishing vessels; freighters passing by; the waves breaking against the unbreakable rocks of the shore; the circling seagulls; the wind and salt blowing over me?

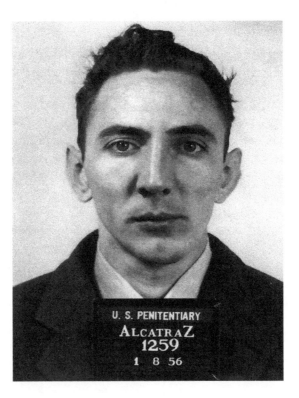

Does such a thing as "dark magic" exist?

Did Robert Johnson – the blues performer who, according to legend, sold his soul to the devil in the 1930's in exchange for becoming the world's best guitar player – possess it?

Does William Garnett Baker?

Maybe it's just a meaningless term. But among the former Alcatraz inmates that are included in this book, one of them is like an unexpected emerald that you find shimmering at the bottom of a bag of rocks.

A *dark* emerald.

Bill Baker is a natural talent who writes brilliant, hard-boiled prose, but you won't find his work in any libraries or bookstores. That's because he used up most of his talent on committing crimes.

Life is short, and Baker has almost consumed his. Yet, he is grateful. He has found love, he is free, he has finally finished the book that he dreamed of writing for so many years.

And, best of all: life still goes on.

***

On September 29, 1958, Aaron Burgett (991-AZ) and Clyde Johnson (864-AZ) over-powered a guard and made their way down to the water. They jumped in and started swimming toward San Francisco. It was a clear day, with no fog to shroud them. Before long, the escape siren sounded and guard-boats plunged into the water. Clyde Johnson got scared and swam back. The guards had him in custody within an hour. Aaron Burgett, however, disappeared without a trace. The city of San Francisco held its collective breath, as several days passed without a clue as to the escaped prisoner's whereabouts.

In my early teens, I wrote a short story about Burgett and Johnson. In a rather pathetic scene, I portrayed the men as weeping just before they staged their escape attempt, filled with the enormity of risking their lives in a dash for freedom.

The reality was not as cinematic as I imagined it from my boy's room in Sweden. Bill Baker knows, because he was one of Aaron Burgett's best friends on Alcatraz, and the day before the escape attempt they said goodbye to each other in the prison yard. A lot like the scene in my story, except no tears were shed.

"Well, I didn't know he would die," Bill says when I call him. "I hoped he would make it."

He describes his friend as "a big, tall, good-looking guy with wide shoulders."

"He worked in the glove shop, where I worked," Bill remembers. "We'd play cards together and stuff like that, we got to know each other pretty well.

Aaron Burgett, 991-AZ

"Aaron was a pretty good guy. He lied a little bit, but of course a lot of people there did. He told us he was in for robbing a bank, but it turned out he was in for robbing a post office. If you robbed a bank, you were respected more."

Sometime in 1958, Burgett decided to attempt the ice-cold swim from Alcatraz to San Francisco. He invited Bill to join him, but he declined.

"I thought about it, but I couldn't figure out how to beat that water," Bill says. "The water kills you. Never mind the sharks, the tides and the current or any of that. It kills you because it's cold. And when I got there I only had three years left. I would have loved to escape, but I'm not suicidal."

Burgett applied to work as a garbage collector so he could carry out his plan. He persuaded Clyde Johnson, who already worked as one, to join him in the escape. The job of collecting garbage around the island meant that both prisoners had freedom of movement, even though they were under a guard's constant supervision.

For two tough men like Burgett and Johnson, overpowering the guard, tying him to a tree and making their way to the water would be the easy part. Swimming to San Francisco, however – that was an insane risk that could cost them their lives:

"I helped Aaron a little bit," Bill says. "I would watch out for guards while he was testing out air-bags in the sink in the bathroom of the glove shop. He would fill them up with air and then push them underwater."

"He was pretty optimistic that he would make it."

On Sunday, September 28, 1958, Burgett approached Bill in the yard.

"He gave me a pack of cigarettes. That was his way of saying that it was time. I hadn't known when he would go, but now I knew," Bill says.

The two friends said their farewells, but they were quiet about it:

"Escape was a very serious thing on Alcatraz. You didn't walk around talking about it. Somebody might overhear you, you just didn't talk about it."

Thirteen days later, Aaron Burgett's bloated, decomposing body was found in San Francisco Bay. Fish and crabs had eaten away much of what was left of him. But he still wore a prison shirt and a belt engraved with the number 991.

In a way, Burgett died a free man. He wasn't locked up when he drew his last breath, even if he was still dressed as a prisoner.

As the days passed without authorities locating Burgett, Bill held out hope that he made it.

Then the announcement came.

"We were locked in our cells when they were searching for him, and it went on for weeks," Bill says. "It was a sad time, of course."

***

William Garnett Baker was born Jan. 25, 1933 and grew up in Kentucky. His parents abandoned him when he was 3 years old, his mother saying she "could not afford" to take care of him. But he lays no blame on them for his becoming a lifelong career criminal.

"My grandmother raised me. She was a good woman, I loved her very much," he says.

Since the age of 16, Bill has spent the vast majority of his life behind bars. When I call him he is 83 years old and has had been a free man for only five years. It wasn't until March 18, 2011 – when he was 78 – that he finally walked out of Leavenworth Prison in Kansas, the last place he did time. When I talk to him, I have difficulty understanding how his life went so wrong.

Bill Baker is no killer. No rapist. No bank robber. Not even a fighter. He comes across as a gentle, thoughtful man who could be working as a librarian.

But he had an almost pathological need to cash fraudulent checks ("I became the best there is", he writes modestly in his book), and his check schemes had him in and out of various prisons from the 1950s onwards.

However, when he came to Alcatraz in early 1957, it was to serve a short sentence for a relatively minor crime:

"I was sentenced to five years for interstate commerce of a stolen automobile, but the reason I was sent to Alcatraz was for escaping from prison. It didn't matter what your sentence was, how long it was or what your original crime was. Everyone who went to Alcatraz – with the exception of a few – were sent there for breaking rules in other prisons. The length of time people spent on Alcatraz were usually three, four or five years," he says.

January 8, 1957, was a foggy day in San Francisco. It was also the day 23-year-old Bill Baker arrived on Alcatraz, booked as prisoner 1259-AZ.

"I was a little scared going there on the boat, I had heard some bad stories about the prison. But it was actually an easy place to do time. It wasn't the best place in the world to be – don't get me wrong, it was a very boring place – but nevertheless we livened it up the best we could. We made a little home-brew once in a while. Maybe we'd bet on ball games and walk the yard and talk about robbing banks and stuff when we got out".

Courtney Taylor, 1038-AZ

Bill didn't know much about check forgery when he arrived at Alcatraz, but he'd be getting an education. One of the prisoners he got to know would play a crucial role in shaping the rest of his criminal life.

"I got to know a guy named Courtney Taylor (1038-AZ) on the island. He was a very intelligent man, and one of the best in the world when it came to check forgery. He taught me – and many others – how to do it," Bill says.

The young man who came to Alcatraz as a mere car thief left after two and a half years as an expert counterfeiter. Bill had a chance to go straight after serving his five-year sentence, but instead, he spent the next five decades committing counterfeiting crimes:

"It was just in my blood or DNA or whatever. That's the way I was. I was wild, I wanted excitement, I liked the money. It was challenging all the time. It was a way of life that I wouldn't recommend for anyone else, but it worked for me", he says.

"I'm like most of the people that were in Alcatraz actually. Because most of the people there did continue with crime when they got out and they served more time in prison. I met guys the rest of my life who had served time on Alcatraz. There weren't that many people that were there, and still you met them in other prisons."

Getting caught over and over again didn't deter him from making more and more phony checks every time he got released. Bill ran like a squirrel in a wheel, clinging to a baseless faith in his own ingenuity, in scheme after scheme. This time, he reasoned, he would stay ahead of the law:

"Us criminals, we're always optimistic – we think we can get away with it the next time," Bill says with a dry laugh.

***

The recreation yard could be the cruelest place on Alcatraz.

Here the prisoners had freedom dangled in front of their faces, so tantalizingly close that they could almost touch it. Sometimes, when the wind was right, they could hear laughter and music coming from the marketplace at Pier 39 alongside Fisherman's Wharf.

The realization that life – *real* life – was happening somewhere close, could be torture for those stuck inside the bleak, rectangular walls of the yard.

One day, Bill decided to lighten the place up. On his way back to his cell from a day's work in the glove factory, he uprooted a small plant and hid it in his pocket. The next day he planted it in the yard, and then cared for it for several weeks. One day in October, he noticed that the plant had begun to blossom. He describes this as his happiest moment on Alcatraz:

"It just felt like the place needed some growth. They had a water faucet out in the yard, so I would water the plant. But this guard, Simmons, he watched over me. He would ask me, 'why do you keep watering that plant?' I said, 'Oh, it's just something to do.'"

But then one day, Bill noticed the plant was gone:

"I was pissed off, of course. Simmons was a very petty guy. Most of the guards weren't like that – they might be mean, but they weren't petty. When they would shake your cell down, they wouldn't bother with the small stuff. Not unless you had a knife or a hack-saw blade of course."

***

The Golden Gate bridge, as seen from the recreation yard on Alcatraz

One of Bill's friends on Alcatraz lost his life during an escape attempt. Another prisoner he got to know – Rufus "Whitey" Franklin (335-AZ) – had killed a guard, many years earlier.

Together with Thomas Limerick (263-AZ) and James Lucas (224-AZ), Franklin beat a guard – Royal C. Cline – to death with a hammer on May 23, 1938. The three men then tried to storm a watchtower on the roof, hoping to steal some guns, then hijack a boat.

But the watchtower guard – Harold Stites – shot Limerick dead and shot and severely injured Franklin. Lucas – who was unscathed – and Franklin were sentenced to life for murdering Cline.

"Whitey was a nice guy. He used to talk about the escape. I don't think he regretted it, but he regretted the failure. And I don't think he would have cried about it to me or anybody else if he did regret it. He may have regretted it secretly, but most people out there didn't get to sniveling," Bill says with a laugh.

"He's one guy I lost track of," he adds after a while.

I tell him that Rufus "Whitey" Franklin was paroled from the federal prison system in 1974 – after almost 40 years behind bars – and that he died of cancer the following year at the age of 59.

"Oh. Well, all my friends from the island are dead," Bill says with melancholy in his voice.

Bill Baker was on the island at the same time as Bob Luke (1118-AZ), but the two prisoners never know each other. Since then, they have both written books about the prison, and they'll sometimes sit side by side in the Alcatraz bookstore, signing autographs.

But the two ex-cons are not close friends. That may be because Bob Luke got out of prison in 1959. while Bill had to wait until 2011.

Rufus Franklin, 335-AZ

"His philosophy on life in general is altogether different from mine. I respect Bob a lot, because he sort of sticks to his guns, he is what he is and that's it. He believes that people have choices, that you can choose not to commit crimes and that's all there is to it. It's either black or white," Bill says.

"I'm just the opposite. I believe that people make choices that make them happy, that they make choices depending on who they are."

One can understand why Bill finds comfort in the notion that we don't control our destinies. After all, he had enough talent to become a book author – but he threw it all away for a life of crime.

Nearly 20 ex-prisoners, and plenty of ex-guards, have written books about their time on the island. "Alcatraz #1259," by Bill Baker, is – in my opinion – the most well-written of them. Bill read a lot in prison and took classes in creative writing. His favorite writer was Zane Grey, a mostly-forgotten American author who wrote adventure novels set in the Wild West.

I tell Bill that his laconic prose reminds me of Elmore Leonard's hard-boiled crime novels.

"Oh, thank you sir," he says.

"That was always a dream for me to write books, and I'd like to write some more. But I'm so busy, and I'm getting old too. I'm working 13 hours a day, five days a week, signing books out on Alcatraz. It takes so long for me to get there. I'm staying in a motel over in Martinez, California, because it's cheaper than living in San Francisco."

Two years after his parole, at 80, Bill married a woman named Mae. He says it's a "challenge" being married, but he seems very much in love. In the dedication of his book, he writes:

When God made Mae He must have dipped her in honey, because she is the sweetest woman in the world.

"This life is more exciting, I meet people from all over the world, and I'm making money legally…I'm okay with it," he says.

I ask Bill if he feels like life gave him a second chance.

"Yes, I do. I'm pretty proud of it, actually," he says, and laughs.

"It's sort of like chasing the American dream. Even though I started out when I was 78."

FIRST DAY ON THE JOB

Monday, May 28, 1951.

As the sun rises on the San Francisco harbor, a 24-year old man with a thick mustache boards a boat bound for Alcatraz. Today will be his first day at work on a new job: prison guard.

"I went to four weeks of good training. They told me to take the weekend off, and to come back Monday morning at 9 o'clock", he recalls.

The new guard is George DeVincenzi. George grew up in an Italian-American neighborhood in San Francisco, then served in the U.S. Navy, at 17 years old, in the final stages of World War II. Working on Alcatraz wasn't considered a desirable job in the early 1950s. The prison housed the most dangerous criminals in the country, yet the starting salary for a guard was only $3,000 a year. But after the war, George had difficulty finding other jobs, so he enrolled in a training course and was hired.

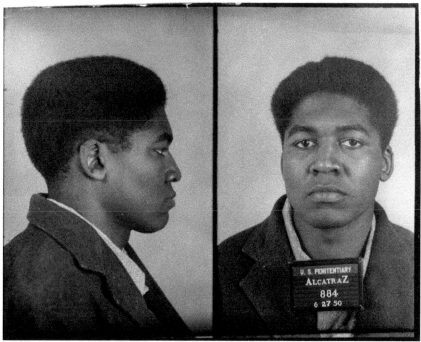

Joseph Barsock, 884-AZ

At 9 a.m. sharp, George checks into work at the big cell house. His first task is guarding prisoners in the barbershop, where a few selected inmates cut other prisoners' hair. Black and white prisoners are segregated on Alcatraz. This morning, it's nine black prisoners' turn at haircuts. One of the inmate barbers is Freddie Lee Thomas (893-AZ), and his first customer of the day is Joseph Barsock (884-AZ).

The two men know each other well – they are, in fact, lovers.

"Thomas cut Barsock, and they started talking," George says.

A few minutes tick by, and George notices the two men having a disagreement about something. The argument escalates quickly – too quickly for him to react.

"After a while they began to speak with louder voices. Suddenly, Thomas took his scissors and stabbed Barsock with them – right in the heart," George says.

"I blew the whistle and threw myself at Thomas. Then he caught me in the leg with the scissors. He wasn't trying to get me, it was an accident. But I got a wound that was over ten inches long".

Other guards rush in, and Freddie Lee Thomas is soon led away. But on his way out, first, he bends down over his boyfriend's dead body.

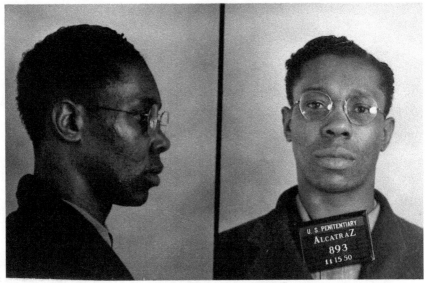

Freddie Lee Thomas, 893-AZ

"I'll never forget it. He bent down over Barsock and said, "I love you". Then he kissed him," George says.

The clock on the wall shows 9:15. George bleeds from his leg and has just witnessed his first murder. He has been working at Alcatraz Penitentiary for exactly fifteen minutes.

"What I thought at that moment?"

George DeVincenzi, now 88 years old, laughs out loud:

"I thought to myself, 'What am I doing here?'"

***

For seven years – from 1951 to 1958 – George DeVincenzi guarded America's worst prisoners. Now he is sitting in a small bookstore in the old Alcatraz cell house. George comes across as a friendly man without a shy fiber in his body, and his eyes twinkle mischievously when he speaks. He laughs happily when tourists want to take a selfie with him, or have their books signed. Suitably – given the story he has just told me – his book is titled "Murders on Alcatraz".

Alcatraz could indeed be a deadly place, and not just for prisoners. In May 1938, the guard Royal C. Cline was killed by inmate Rufus "Whitey" Franklin (335-AZ) during an escape attempt. Eight years later, two other guards – William A. Miller and Harold P. Stites – were killed during the bloody "Battle of Alcatraz". But George shakes his head when I ask him if the threat of violence was the worst thing about working on Alcatraz:

"No. That wasn't an everyday occurrence. My biggest challenge was the monotony. You stood locked up in the gun galleries and the towers for eight hours, without anything to do," he says.

George's friendly manner made him popular with most prisoners - sometimes *too* popular.

"There was one guy who grew up in San Francisco, five, six blocks from my home. He tried to get close to me, wanted to know which church I went to and so on. I told him that we couldn't get close. Because they could take advantage of you then," he says.

George DeVincenzi signing his book on Alcatraz, 2015

Some prisoners George oversaw were more infamous than others. Robert Stroud (594-AZ), a convicted murderer, is known to history as the "Birdman of Alcatraz." Stroud was a respected expert on bird diseases and wrote books about it while in prison. (He never had any birds in his cell on Alcatraz, though. That was forbidden.) Hollywood made a movie about him in 1962, with Burt Lancaster in the starring role. Lancaster portrayed him as a kindly gentleman, but in reality, he was a mentally-disturbed double murderer who, during his 17 years on Alcatraz, had to be kept separate from other prisoners because of his bizarre behavior.

""The warden's requirement was, if you take Stroud out of his cell, everyone has to be locked up. Many didn't like that, but that's the way the warden wanted it," George says.

"He was a psychopath. I got to know him very well. He was up in the hospital in a special cell. We used to play checkers, even though it was against the rules for me to do that."

One of George's duties was keeping an eye on Stroud while he took his weekly baths.

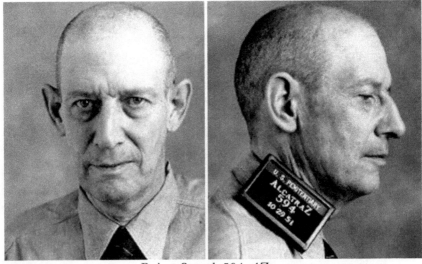

Robert Stroud, 594-AZ

"He'd take a bath for about an hour and a half, while another officer was shaking his cell down. He had attempted suicide twice. I would say, 'Robert, get out of there. I gotta go to lunch!'

"He'd say, 'Oh, give me few more minutes. I'll get up.' I always gave him a few more minutes....”

“We gave him a locked razor, so he couldn’t get the blade out,” George says. “Robert shaved his face, shaved his head, and shaved his body. Don’t ask me why, but that’s what he did.”

Another infamous prisoner was Clarence Carnes (714-AZ), who arrived on Alcatraz in 1945 at age 18 after a murder conviction. Carnes would have committed a second murder on the island had George not stopped him.

“You know how kids in school make paper kites? One day, one came flying down from the third floor of B block and went right by me. I picked it up, and it was a note that said, ‘Carnes is going to kill Johnson. He’s got a knife,’ George recalls.

“We went to Carnes,” George recalled. “He had a big knife in his cell, six inches, made out of copper. But we never did find out who Johnson was. There were three or four prisoners with that name.” George left the prison system in 1959 and worked for the U.S. Customs Service until his retirement. But he still returns to his old workplace on Alcatraz to tell stories.

“The first time I came back here, it was kind of an odd feeling. I’d look around, and remember everything,” he says.

George laughs, smiling for another selfie, this one for a Japanese tourist.

“But I don’t feel like that anymore. I’ve been doing this for 30 years now,” he continues.

During my visit, several people ask him how guards treated prisoners on the island. Some tourists probably go to Alcatraz with pictures images of the fictional “Hellcatraz” in their minds. The jovial nature of George DeVincenzi doesn’t fit the cliché of the sadistic guard.

But when I ask him about the "Hole" – the cold, dark cells of cellblock D, the ultimate punishment for unruly prisoners – George suddenly acts nonchalant. From a modern point of view, such punishment is akin to torture. Naked prisoners not seeing daylight for up to 19 days, freezing on a cold concrete floor, and barely getting any food. Some prisoners have testified that, after going days without any sense of time or space, they suffered from such severe anxiety that they hallucinated inside the darkened cells.

But when I ask George if, in hindsight, he views the punishment method as inhumane, he dismisses my question with an irritated wave of his hand.

"No, not really. The doctor would check on them every day, and every third day they'd be given somewhat of a small meal. The rest of the time they got bread and water", he says.

But how did they act when you released them after 19 days? I ask.

"Oh, they were good boys then! No smoking, hardly any food, locked up in that hole there...they behaved after that", George says.

And then his hearty laughter echoes between the thick, concrete walls of the old cell house.

1441-AZ, 1476-AZ, 1485-AZ

What happened on the night between 11 and 12 June 1962, meant the end of Alcatraz. When news broke that three prisoners had disappeared without a trace, the image of the prison as being escape-proof was shattered. Attorney General Robert Kennedy closed its doors only nine months later. There were other reasons why the prison was shut down, it was too expensive to operate and the cell house was in urgent need of a renovation, but the amazing feat of Frank Morris and the Anglin brothers sped up the process considerably.

Paradoxically, the escape also meant that another Alcatraz was born – the mythological Alcatraz. Without it, Clint Eastwood would not have made a classic movie about the prison in 1979. Without it, a drove of books, films, television documentaries and newspaper articles would not have been produced over the years. Most of them centered around the same question: did the "Escape from Alcatraz"-trio make it?

And if so, are they still alive today?

Would Alcatraz even be a museum today if it wasn't for the escape – and if so, would it attract over a million visitors a year?

Over half a century later, the escape of 1962 still tops major news sites on a regular basis. Like when it celebrated its 50th anniversary in 2012. Or when the television documentary "Alcatraz: Search for the truth" premiered on the History Channel in the fall of 2015, and presented a photograph that allegedly shows two of the prisoners in Brazil, thirteen years after they disappeared. The "news" was given a great deal of attention by media outlets around the world.

Almost all of the prisoners I have interviewed in this book have something to say about the escape. One of them even claims to know for sure what happened to the three escapees, but it's impossible to authenticate his story.

One thing is clear: Frank Morris and the Anglin brothers belong in a book about the last survivors of the prison. For even if they died in the escape, they made sure that Alcatraz lives on to this day.

***

It says "crap" on a folder.

Michael Dyke explains why:

"Here is where I collect the craziest leads I get. People who claim that Clarence Anglin is their father, stuff like that. Things that can't possibly be true."

Outside the window, central Oakland is in full spring bloom. A mug of coffee sits next to a computer on a desktop littered with papers. Michael Dyke, a burly, bearded man, invites me in and offers me a glass of water. It is from this tiny office in a tall US Marshals building that Dyke conducts the world's most famous fugitive hunt:

"We will conduct an active investigation until the men reach the age of 99," he says.

Until December 31, 1979, the FBI ran the investigation, but these days the US Marshals Services are in charge. Michael Dyke has been the chief investigator since 2003, and it is far from the only case he is working on – even if it's the only one that is world famous. When the escape celebrated its 50-year anniversary in 2012 he was forced to do interviews with several national TV shows, as well as with media from all over the world.

But he doesn't like it when the case is back in the news:

"I actually don't care for the case to be in the news, because it draws out people who make erroneous reports about them and that makes the investigation more time consuming than it already is," he says.

Michael Dyke in his Oakland office, 2015

It's May of 2015 when I pay him a visit. 53 years has passed since Frank Morris, 35, John Anglin, 32, and Clarence Anglin, 31, disappeared from Alcatraz without a trace. Still, Michael Dyke believes there is a small chance that they made it:

"Statistically speaking, two out of every three bodies that drowned in San Francisco Bay during the 1960's were eventually recovered. That all three would have disappeared is a little bit strange," he says.

Every now and then, a possible lead has given the investigation new life. A few years ago, Dyke received a tip from a person in the Midwest:

"It looked like we had found John Anglin. I was sent a photo of an elderly man: the age was about right, and it really looked like him.

And the man in question was actually named John Anglin!"

The chief investigator enjoyed a brief moment of hope: could this finally be the breakthrough he had been waiting for? He shows me the picture of the man. The similarity between this John Anglin, and the FBI-manipulated, age-progressed mugshot of the former Alcatraz prisoner of the same name, is striking.

But like all other leads, it turned out to be a dead end:

"We sent out an agent, and the man could prove that he wasn't John Anglin from Alcatraz. He had a big birthmark on one of his legs, which the other John Anglin didn't have. They were not even related, it was just a big coincidence that they had the same name," Dyke says.

In recent years, new theories have been introduced in various television documentaries, such as a raft that was supposedly found on nearby Angel Island the day after the escape – indicating that the three men had managed to cross the water.

"I have reviewed a lot of police reports and memorandums from 1962, and it is true that a raft on Angel Island is mentioned in one of them. But the raft is not mentioned elsewhere, and the report does not specify what it looked like. So it could have been any type of object made of rubber," Michael Dyke says.

Reports that a car was stolen in the area by three men during the night of the escape, or that the Anglin brothers appeared at their mother's funeral a few years later – dressed as women, to avoid discovery – is nonsense, according to Dyke.

Another, more plausible lead, is a Norwegian cargo ship named *SS Norefjell*, whose crew saw something floating in the water about three miles northwest of the Golden Gate bridge on July 17, 1962. In their report to the FBI, the crew described the object as "a human body floating face down in the water ", but they were unable to pick it up.

Half a year later, skeletal remains were found on a nearby beach. They were never identified, but in 2011 the remains were dug up for the National Geographic documentary "Vanished from Alcatraz".

"I participated in that documentary. By investigating the remains, we found that they belonged to a man that had been of exactly the same length as Frank Morris. We obtained DNA samples from a relative of his, but they did not match with the body," says Michael Dyke.

However, he has not given up hope that the body may actually be that of Frank Morris – the relative who left a DNA test came from Frank's father's side, and it is unclear who his biological father really was.

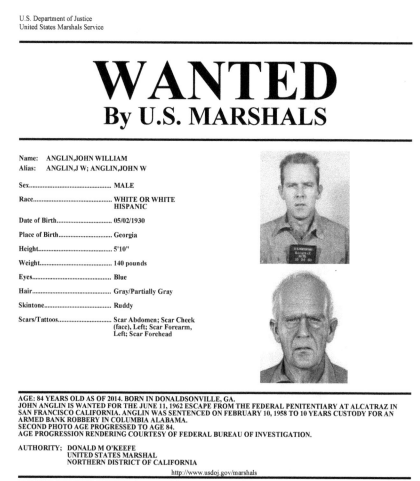

U.S. Department of Justice
United States Marshals Service

WANTED
By U.S. MARSHALS

Name: ANGLIN,JOHN WILLIAM
Alias: ANGLIN,J W; ANGLIN,JOHN W

Sex.................................. MALE

Race................................ WHITE OR WHITE HISPANIC

Date of Birth...................... 05/02/1930

Place of Birth..................... Georgia

Height.............................. 5'10"

Weight.............................. 140 pounds

Eyes................................. Blue

Hair.................................. Gray/Partially Gray

Skintone............................ Ruddy

Scars/Tattoos..................... Scar Abdomen; Scar Cheek (face), Left; Scar Forearm, Left; Scar Forehead

AGE: 84 YEARS OLD AS OF 2014. BORN IN DONALDSONVILLE, GA.
JOHN ANGLIN IS WANTED FOR THE JUNE 11, 1962 ESCAPE FROM THE FEDERAL PENITENTIARY AT ALCATRAZ IN SAN FRANCISCO CALIFORNIA. ANGLIN WAS SENTENCED ON FEBRUARY 10, 1958 TO 10 YEARS CUSTODY FOR AN ARMED BANK ROBBERY IN COLUMBIA ALABAMA.
SECOND PHOTO AGE PROGRESSED TO AGE 84.
AGE PROGRESSION RENDERING COURTESY OF FEDERAL BUREAU OF INVESTIGATION.

AUTHORITY; DONALD M O'KEEFE
UNITED STATES MARSHAL
NORTHERN DISTRICT OF CALIFORNIA

http://www.usdoj.gov/marshals

NOTICE TO ARRESTING AGENCY: Before arrest, validate warrant through National Crime Information Center (NCIC). If arrested or whereabouts known, contact the nearest United States Marshals Office or call the United States Marshals Service Headquarters at 1-877-926-8332.

US Marshals wanted poster for John Anglin

To find this out, Michael Dyke has been working like a modern-day Sherlock Holmes – scouring various archives for marriage certificates and birth announcements from the 1920s:

"If I can determine who Frank Morris's biological father really was, I can also find relatives that can be compared to a DNA test of the body we dug up. This is the closest I've come," he sighs and shows me a wedding ad from a local newspaper.

"It's from 1926, the same year Frank was born, and it shows that a man named Eddie Morris married his mother. But Eddie Morris is not listed on the birth certificate – another man is. Eddie Morris abandoned Frank's mother when Frank was little, and then he vanished. I think he was the biological father, but it's impossible to say for sure," Michael Dyke says.

A wedding ad from 1926 is certainly not much of a lead – but for a long time that was all Michael Dyke had.

***

Ken Widner, 54, was just a baby – and his brother David, 48, wasn't even born – when their uncles John and Clarence Anglin entered the history books. Their mother Marie – John's and Clarence's little sister – heard the news of the escape on the radio on the morning of June 12, 1962. After that, their lives were turned upside down: The Widner brothers claim the FBI harassed their family by bugging their phones and turning up unannounced for sudden cross-examinations regarding the escapees.

But they never said anything about what they knew. Not until the autumn of 2015, that is.

Five months after my meeting with chief investigator Dyke in Oakland, Ken and David Widner were the reason why the infamous cold case made headlines all over again. That's when they participated in a television documentary on the History Channel, and presented a previously unknown photograph. It allegedly shows John and Clarence in Brazil in 1975, alive and free. The image got a lot of exposure in both U.S. and international media, since it would prove at least two of the prisoners actually made it to freedom.

"The family has known for a long time that John and Clarence made it, that's not something we realized just now. But it took a long time before we could trust someone in law enforcement enough to show them what we knew. And this is a test for the police too; now let's see if we can really trust them. Before we can lead the police to where we think they are, we want to be sure they don't put handcuffs on our uncles," David Widner says.

The two brothers are happy and talkative when I call them in November 2015. They are obviously proud of their famous uncles, and think were disrespectfully portrayed in the Clint Eastwood movie "Escape from Alcatraz":

"We would love to see a remake of that movie, that tells the story of how the escape really happened. In the movie Frank Morris gets all the credit, but if you read the FBI's investigation of the escape they were completely amazed by how inventive John and Clarence were. They could make things out of nothing," Ken Widner says.

"What is the first thing you would say to your uncles, if you were to meet them?" I ask.

The other end of the line suddenly falls silent.

***

We may never know exactly how the story of the "Escape from Alcatraz" will end. But we do know that the first chapter of the long and sensational saga was written in 1958, when a man named Allen Clayton West arrived on the island.

West's background was predictably tragic. He grew up in a broken family with alcoholic parents and began his crime career as a child stealing cars. When he was 14 years old he was sent to a youth detention center in Georgia. After that he committed various burglaries around the country and went in and out of prison. In 1957 he tried to escape from Florida State Prison, threatening the warden with a gun. The following year he was sent to Alcatraz as prisoner 1335-AZ. That was to be his second stint on the island; a few years earlier, he had served another sentence on "The Rock" as prisoner 1130-AZ.

On January 18, 1960, Frank Lee Morris arrived on the island and was booked as prisoner 1441-AZ. He was a short, muscular man with intense, blue eyes, and his background was in many ways a carbon copy of Allen Wests; a broken childhood home led to a career in crime, that started with a burglary at the age of 13 and escalated to bank robberies and drug smuggling.

Allen West, 1335-AZ

But Morris was smarter than West. In his prison file, a psychologist had described his intellect as "superior", and his IQ was measured at 133 – a figure that only about two percent of the general population reach under the so-called Wechsler scale.

Despite his intelligence, Morris was a failed criminal who had been in prison for 18 of the last 20 years when he arrived on Alcatraz. However, he had a natural talent to escape, and that was what got him sent to Alcatraz.

Escape artist, he was called in the file – a title he was soon to live up to.

On October 24, 1960, John William Anglin was sent to Alcatraz, and three months later his little brother Clarence joined him.

The Anglin brothers came from a poor family in Ruskin, Florida, as middle children in a brood of fourteen. Together with their older brother Alfred they started robbing banks in the mid-1950s. One such robbery – in the sleepy town of Columbia, Alabama in 1958 – netted them $19,000, but they were captured only four days later as they lay sleeping in their van. Clarence and Alfred were sentenced to 15 years behind bars, John to ten. When John and Clarence unsuccessfully attempted to escape from Leavenworth prison in Kansas, they bought their ticket to "The Rock". John became prisoner 1476-AZ, Clarence 1485-AZ.

John – "J.W" or "J-Dub" as he was called – was a bit of a dreamer who, even though he was one year older than Clarence, looked up to his little brother.

(US Marshals wanted poster of Frank Morris)

"I liked Clarence the best out of the two brothers. We became really good friends. Clarence was a soft-spoken guy who was easy to talk to. He wasn't the brightest guy, but I liked him," former Alcatraz inmate Bob Schibline (1355-AZ) says.

"I didn't know John as well, but I liked both of the Anglin brothers. Frank Morris, on the other hand, I didn't get along with at all. We were like cats and dogs and argued all the time. He had a high IQ, I had a high IQ, we were both alpha males...we just didn't get along."

***

As early as the late 1950s, Allen West had formed a plan:

"I heard about West's plan long before the three who later escaped had even arrived on the island," says Harvey Carignan (935-AZ).

West was an energetic man who constantly babbled about his masterplan to everybody who wanted to listen. Some prisoners did so with interest, but most rejected his plan as unrealistic:

"For West, it was all about putting together the right group of men. He asked me once if I ever thought of escaping, and when I told him that I didn't, he never mentioned it again. This was in about 1960, and the reason he asked me was because he thought I was serving a life sentence, but I wasn't," says Harvey Carignan.

Another ex-inmate who listened to West's talk was Frank Sprenz (1414-AZ):

"West was the architect and engineer behind the Morris/Anglin escape. He was the one assigned to clean the utility service area behind the blocks, and he was the one who noticed the concrete behind the cell wall was weakened. It was his idea to excavate under the sinks from behind. He also was on top of the three-tiered B block and found the barred three-foot-wide vent in the ceiling," Sprenz says.

The Department of Prisons had been struggling with a tight budget for a number of years. With a main building that was over 50 years old, Alcatraz was in dire need of a renovation but there was simply no money for it.

Therefore, the pipes in the ancient sewage system often broke, leading saltwater from San Francisco Bay to seep into the utility corridors behind the cells. There it slowly made the cement in the walls soft and porous.

The strained budget also forced the prison management to begin to compromise with the very thing that had always been Alcatraz's strength: the tight security. A guard tower on the roof of the prison was left unmanned during nighttime. During 1961, the total guard force was reduced from 98 to 91 men.

Sometime during '61, Allen West had convinced both Frank Morris and the Anglin brothers that his plan was feasible. Step one was to get out of the cells. The only possible way was to go through the ventilation duct openings under the sinks at the back of the cells, and West had noticed that the old concrete had become so porous that it was possible to scrape away crumbs with a fingernail.

WANTED
By U.S. MARSHALS

Name: ANGLIN, CLARENCE
Alias: MILLER, CARL WILLIAM

Sex................................... MALE

Race................................. WHITE OR WHITE
                                      HISPANIC

Date of Birth.................... 05/11/1931

Place of Birth................... Georgia

Height.............................. 5'11"

Weight.............................. 168 pounds

Eyes................................. Hazel

Hair.................................. Gray/Partially Gray

Scars/Tattoos.................... Scar Arm, Right Upper;
                                   Scar Lip, Upper; Tattoo
                                   Arm, Right Upper; Tattoo
                                   Forearm, Left

AGE: 83 YEARS OLD AS OF 2014.
CLARENCE ANGLIN IS WANTED FOR THE JUNE 11, 1962 ESCAPE FROM THE FEDERAL PENITENTIARY AT
ALCATRAZ, SAN FRANCISCO CALIFORNIA. ANGLIN WAS SENTENCED ON FEBRUARY 10, 1958 TO 15 YEARS CUSTODY
FOR AN ARMED BANK ROBBERY IN COLUMBIA ALABAMA. TATTOOS: "ZONA" L-ARM & "NITA" R-ARM.
SECOND PHOTO AGE PROGRESSED TO AGE 84.
AGE PROGRESSION RENDERING COURTESY OF FEDERAL BUREAU OF INVESTIGATION.

AUTHORITY; DONALD M O'KEEFE
            UNITED STATES MARSHAL
            NORTHERN DISTRICT OF CALIFORNIA
            http://www.usdoj.gov/marshals

NOTICE TO ARRESTING AGENCY: Before arrest, validate warrant through National Crime Information Center (NCIC). If arrested or
whereabouts known, contact the nearest United States Marshals Office or call the United States Marshals Service Headquarters at
1-877-926-8332.

US Marshals wanted poster of Clarence Anglin

With handles from spoons that had been broken off and sharpened, the four prisoners began to dig small, round holes in a square pattern around the duct openings. After they had made their way around, they were able to simply kick the entire brick into the utility corridor on the other side of the wall. In order to camouflage the holes, the men put pieces of toilet paper in them and painted them with watercolors. When work was completed they could barely squirm out of the holes.

The four men also managed to construct a simple electric drill, using an old broken vacuum engine that was smuggled to them by another prisoner. But using it meant taking an extreme risk, because it made so much noise:

"Some of us would holler and talk extra loud to conceal the sound of the drill. Some even played the harmonica," Bob Schibline says.

The next step was to get out of the prison building itself. West had heard of the old ventilation shafts in the ceiling of the cell house. There were eight of them, all in all, but most were no longer in use. The guards had sealed many of them with cement, but one of the drums above the corner of cell block B was still open. A way out suddenly seemed within reach: If they could get up to the top of the cell block in the middle of the night and saw past the bars, climb through the ventilation shaft, kick out the hood and get up on the roof, slide down the smoke stack that ran along the cell building, get down to the water...

But there were several problems. One of the biggest obstacles they faced was that the guards counted the prisoners on Alcatraz in their cells at regular intervals – even at night. Even though the four men managed to get out of their cells and make their way up on the roof, it wouldn't be long before their absence was discovered.

The solution was to create real-life looking dummy heads that could be put on the pillows in the cells and thus fool the guards. By soaking bits of toilet paper, mixing them with soap, glue, and leftover cement from the holes in the cells, the men created lumps of mass which they then shaped into human heads. When the heads had dried, they painted red mouths on them and used a skin-like color for the rest of the face.

"John and Clarence made beautiful paintings of their girlfriends. The reason they did that was to get paint that they could use on the dummy heads," says their nephew Ken Widner, who is still in possession of the paintings in question.

Clarence Anglin worked as a barber and stuffed his pockets full of hair from freshly cut prisoners. The dummy heads soon had impressively thick, wavy hair on their scalps. The four prisoners even took the time to make eyebrows and eyelashes.

***

Behind the cells was a narrow and dark utility corridor filled with the thick, rusty pipes that was Alcatraz's aging sewage system. The corridor stretched right up to the ceiling, and it would be easy for the men to get up to the top of the cell block; the winding sewage system was like a natural ladder of sorts.

The ventilation drum in the ceiling was fitted with two sets of bars. The first one was small and could be bent, but the second one was thicker. It was attached to the drum with twelve bolts, but the bolts were small and could be sawed through using a metal file that the men received from an inmate working in the industry building.

The prisoners would, however, be completely exposed to the watchful eyes of the guard in the gun gallery during the time-consuming work of sawing through the bolts. Again, West thought of a brilliant solution. He offered to paint the ceiling, and asked the guards for permission to hang up blankets on the cell bars at the top of the cell house in order to prevent the spread of dirt and paint residues. Unbelievably, Deputy Warden Art Dollison agreed to this, and with the blankets in place, West, Morris and the Anglin brothers could take turns at sawing away at the bolts in the ventilation drum without risk of being detected.

There was one big obstacle left, of course. The biggest of them all.

The cold and treacherous San Francisco Bay still stood between the four men and their freedom.

***

The prisoners planned – and Bob Schibline listened.

He had no other choice, because his cell was on the ground floor of B-block just like the others, which meant that they sat at the same table in the large mess hall for breakfast, lunch and dinner:

"We had ten-men tables in the dining room. There weren't a lot of people on the first floor, because it was very cold. You had to ask to be moved up to an upper floor, but I was a rebel – if somebody said "black", I'd holler "white!". I refused to ask them any favors," Bob says.

One day at breakfast, West, Morris and the Anglin brothers suddenly spoke Spanish at the table, and Bob was impressed:

"I said: 'whoa, you're taking up Spanish fast! You speak like natives!'. The guy next to me said: 'So where are you heading to, South America?'. They said something about Argentina or Brazil, and I said: "But in Brazil, they speak Portuguese, bot Spanish.' Then they said: 'Well, it's close enough.'"

The problem of crossing San Francisco Bay was widely discussed. Bob was involved in the talks, but decided not to join the escape:

"I only had five years left of my sentence, so I wasn't about to throw myself into the water," Bob explains.

To merely try to swim to the mainland was considered too dangerous. Four years earlier, prisoner Aaron Burgett (991-AZ) had become the latest proof of this when he drowned in the Bay on his way to freedom.

Again, the solution was to seek help from other Alcatraz cons. Numerous prisoners – exactly how many have never been completely established, but at least several dozen – knew of the plan, and helped the men by smuggling tools and items out of the various workplaces on the island. That was their way of contributing to the escape. If they could not join in it themselves – at least they could avenge the hated prison by helping the escapees.

"They stole some rain coats from storage to make rafts. And an accordion, to make a pump for the rafts," says Jerry Clymore (1339-AZ).

The "prison code" – helping a fellow con, no matter what – was unusually strong on Alcatraz, according to James "Whitey" Bulger (1428-AZ):

"In no other prison in the world could four men work for almost a year, dig through stone and steel, crawl, climb and swim to safety, and have at least twenty other prisoners be aware of the plan and help them. And no one traded the info for parole or transfer," Bulger writes in a letter.

The manufacturing of simple life vests was soon underway. Safely hidden behind the blankets that Allen West had hung at the top of cell block B, the prisoners also took turn to sew together a crude raft that they hoped would be sturdy enough to carry them to freedom.

Bob Schibline was an experienced scuba diver, and told his friends that they were better off skipping the rafts in favor of another, easier solution:

"I told Frank Morris: "The best thing to do is to get some of these surgical gloves, put them inside your shirt, and use them for buoyancy. But Frank was an egotistical son of a bitch. He had his own way of doing things and nothing I said moved him whatsoever," Bob says.

It wasn't just the cold water that presented a problem. There was also a risk that the powerful, fast currents of San Francisco Bay would carry the men out to the Pacific Ocean instead of the mainland, regardless of how hard they paddled or swam. Bob Schibline worked down in the docks, and one day he came up with a way to give his friends some extra information that could prove invaluable:

"One of the guards would bring a newspaper there, which was against the law. The paper had the tide tables in them. I had access to the guards' newspaper, which was in the dock office, but I could not get them every day. I was lucky to get them three times a week, most of the time it was just twice a week," Bob says.

"The last tide table I got was from Friday's paper, and I gave it to Clarence on Saturday in the yard. The next day, Sunday, Morris came up to me in the yard, and said: 'We appreciate you getting us the tide table, but regardless of the tide, we plan to leave when we get to the water and have everything inflated.' I looked at him in stunned silence. I could not believe that he didn't think knowledge of the tide table was important."

Monday evening, Bob sat in the mess hall with the four soon-to-be fugitives and ate dinner with them for the very last time.

"The good-byes weren't emotional; these were my fellow cons and not my best friends. Besides, deep down in my heart, I didn't think they would ever get off the island and that I would see them again when they got out of the Hole."

***

The lights in the cell house were turned off at 9.30 pm on June 11, 1962.

In cells B-138 (Morris), B-140 (West), B-150 (John Anglin) and B-152 (Clarence Anglin), the four men got ready. They placed the dummy heads in the beds and began to crawl out of their cells.

But right away there was a problem – Allen West wasn't able to make it out of the hole in his cell:

"He claimed there was a piece of steel in front of the hole that he hadn't noticed before," Bob Schibline says.

West began to dig frenetically in order to get rid of the steel rod, and he probably got help from the other side of the vent by Morris. But the clock was ticking, and the other three prisoners soon had no other choice but to leave him behind.

It was indeed a cruel fate. The architect and the mastermind of the escape, who had spent years of careful planning and recruiting, did not get a shot at freedom himself.

Or? Bob Schibline believes that Allen West simply got cold feet:

"I didn't trust West very much. I think he had second thoughts about the plan, and chose to remain on the island," Bob says.

Regardless of which, it was now up to Frank Morris and the Anglin brothers to continue on their own. They climbed to the top of the cell house. There they picked up their life jackets, paddles, their raft – even a crude pump to blow it up with, made of an old accordion – and pushed the hood of the ventilation drum onto the roof from below to get out of the cell house.

"That night we all heard them when they hit the roof. That big vent cover hit the roof with a loud clang, and all the seagulls that were so startled into wakefulness made such a clamor that even guards called in to report all the noise. At that point, I thought: 'That's the ball game!' But I believe that the guards were so convinced in their own propaganda. In their minds, if the head count was ok – then who cares about some noise," Bob Schibline says.

He held his breath, waiting to hear prompt footsteps from guards, followed by the sound of the escape siren. In cell C-310, "Whitey" Bulger felt the same dread:

"The gulls that rested on the roof made a loud, squeaking noise. We leapt out of our beds and started making noises to confuse the night cell house guard," he recalls.

It worked. No one seemed to notice the sounds coming from the roof, and after a while the seagulls stopped their screaming.

The three men ran over the roof of the prison in the dark night. Above the hospital area they stopped, and made their way down from the tall building via a large smoke stack. This caused a lot of soot to accumulate on the ground, and on the FBI photographs taken the following day, black footprints can be seen moving towards the water.

*∗∗

Nobody knows for sure whether Allen West got cold feet – as Bob Schibline suggests – or if he really was unable to leave his cell. West died of acute peritonitis in a Florida prison in 1978. It's possible that he actually planned to escape, for several hours after his companions had left he finally managed to get out of his cell and make his way up on the roof.

At that time, Allen West must have felt like the loneliest man in the world. There he was, on top of America's most notorious prison, feeling the cool breeze of the Bay against his face. The San Francisco skyline glittered like a Christmas tree in the night, and if the escape had gone according to plan, his three friends were out there now, somewhere in the darkness.

Free men, all three of them.

But West never jumped in the water to try and join them:

"On the night of the escape he was on the roof, but the bad weather and high waves surpassed his daring and nerve so he returned to his cell," Frank Sprenz says.

"That's exactly what happened – from West himself."

*∗∗

In cell B-110, Bob Schibline closed his eyes and dozed off for a few hours.

"I fell asleep. In the morning I woke up by the morning bell, and we stood up by the bars to get counted as usual," Bob says.

What followed is one of the most tragicomic and dramatic moments in prison history. One of the most famous scenes in Clint Eastwood's "Escape from Alcatraz" – the moment that the guards notice that Clint & Co has disappeared without a trace during the night – transpired in almost exactly the same way in real life, it turns out.

Bob Schibline knows, because he was one of the very few prisoners who were in a position to witness everything from his cell at the bottom of the large cell house corridor that the prisoners had dubbed "Broadway". By holding out a mirror through the bars he was able to see how one of the guards slowly approached Frank Morris cell – and then stopped:

"He said "Come on Morris, get up!" Nothing happened. Finally he reached in with his hand in to shake Franks head, and the head rolled down on the floor! He must have jumped back about three or four feet. He said: "Oh my God!" and started to blow his little stupid whistle," Bob says.

It was a triumphant moment for all the prisoners – probably hundreds, all in all – who knew about the escape for months and had pulled for their friends Frank, John and Clarence to make it. It is possible to hear the smile in Bob Schibline's voice when he remembers the exact moment when all the excitement and nervousness gave way to euphoria:

"When the whistle blew, everybody broke into cheers. The whole prison just erupted!"

James "Whitey" Bulger was one of many who joined in the celebration:

"We let out cheers and screams of joy. It was the happiest moment I can ever remember."

***

Warden Olin G. Blackwell was on vacation. In his place, Deputy warden Arthur M. "Art" Dollison was acting warden of Alcatraz, and it was at the Dollison family house that the phone rang shortly after 7:00 am on June 12.

Art Dollison's daughter, Jolene, was fifteen years old that day. She lived on the island with her parents and two siblings, and lay asleep in her room upstairs when an unexpected noise disturbed her dreams:

"I had never heard the siren before. We had lived there 1954 through 1955 when I was a little girl, but I had never heard the siren. It was loud! It woke me up. Your first thought is, 'This can't be an escape attempt,' even though you know that it is," Jolene says.

"I grabbed my robe and ran downstairs, my mother was coming up the stairs. "Get dressed," she said, "There's been an escape." She wasn't scared and we both figured they had left the island the night before," she continues.

Art Dollison rushed up to the prison building and was informed that the impossible had happened – three prisoners had disappeared without a trace during the night.

But where had they gone? Jolene and her mother were seized by a moment's panic:

"We did search the house and there was a moment when we had to go into the basement when neither one of us wanted to ascend the stairs first. It was dark and cut out of rock, so I'm sure it was unfinished in places. It also had darker rooms beyond the main dark room. And, more importantly, it had an outside entrance. So if anybody was hiding on the island, this could potentially be one of those places," Jolene remembers.

"I ran and got a paring knife. It's an apple peeler, it's the shortest knife in the kitchen, and she laughed at me. But I'd had thought about it on the way to the kitchen: I didn't want a butcher knife! I explained that I figured I wouldn't get hurt if someone took from me. Nobody was down there. Jean Long came over a few minutes later. She was the island post master. Fun lady, big laugh, lived there nine years with her two kids. Mom fixed a pot of coffee, I had hot chocolate and we sat in the dining room and swapped stories."

Art Dollison had a long and solid career in the prison system behind him. Now – with just three years left until his retirement – he was suddenly acting warden for a prison that had been humiliated in front of the entire world. The sensational news soon broke, and Dollison (as well as Blackwell, who was called back from his vacation) were forced to hold press conferences where they tried to explain how the mighty Alcatraz could have been broken by three small time criminals.

I ask Jolene how her dad was affected by all this. How did it feel to be held responsible for such a total failure?

"Well I really don't know. I mean, I never asked him about his feelings. But it triggered a minor heart attack that summer. So I'm sure he held that close to his chest, as they say. I don't think he took it as a personal failure," she says.

Within a few days, the search for the escapees had grown to be the largest police hunt in San Francisco's history, but it led nowhere.

"We could hear explosions when they threw hand grenades in the caves on the island, to make sure nobody was hiding there," Bob Schibline says.

Allen West was detained and admitted his role in the escape:

"They moved him to D-block, where I sat at the time. Then he was transferred, and we never saw him again," Jerry Clymore says.

On the night of June 12, a wooden paddle was found floating in the water close to the neighboring Angel Island, and two days later a plastic pocket was found in the same area. It belonged to Clarence Anglin, and contained over seventy photographs of his relatives and friends. On June 15, a life jacket was found three miles north of the Golden Gate, and on June 22, another one was found roughly a hundred yards from Alcatraz. Both were punctured and water-filled.

Jolene Dollison is now called Jolene Babyak, and has written the book "Breaking the Rock" about the escape. She belongs to those who are convinced that the three men drowned in the water:

"Many who have studied the escape are convinced that they didn't make it. They were very poor men, and would have needed a lot of help from the outside. Someone would have had to pick them up with a boat, and then drive or fly them out of the country. That would have cost a lot of money that they simply didn't have," she says.

In her book, Jolene Babyak describes the Anglin brothers as poorly educated, boastful and unintelligent. When I point out that their nephews are annoyed over the fact that their uncles usually don't get much credit for planning the ingenious escape, she lets out a laugh:

"I know the family doesn't like how John and Clarence have been portrayed throughout the years, but that's the way they were. The brothers weren't the masterminds behind the escape. John arrived on Alcatraz in October of 1960, Clarence in the beginning of 1961. They were latecomers, and weren't involved in the planning. That was mostly West's doing. And maybe Morris's, he was undoubtedly a smart man," Jolene Babyak says.

***

It is unclear whether the escapees ever actually intended to swim or even paddle to the mainland. In the History Channel documentary "Alcatraz: Search for the truth", the Anglins' nephews Ken and David Widner put forth the theory that the three men first made their way around the whole island to the dock area. According to the theory, they then waited for several hours for the night ferry to arrive. The ferry departed at 00.10 that night, and by tying a long electric cable from their raft to the rudder of the boat they could have been towed to the mainland.

Bob Schibline doesn't buy that theory:

"I would have noticed if there was a wire missing down in the docks, I was in charge of that stuff. I think there's somebody else in that picture. I think they died," he says.

But Ken and David Widner are sure of their case. According to them, their uncles and Frank Morris got help from someone on the outside to reach the mainland – and then went to Brazil. There they settled in the countryside and lived an anonymous life as farmers.

The reason they believe this is because a man named Fred Brizzi - a childhood friend of the Anglin brothers - contacted the family in 1992 and told them a sensational story. Brizzi claimed that he accidentally met John and Clarence in a bar outside Rio de Janeiro in 1975. His old childhood friends then invited him to the farm where they lived, and willingly posed for a picture.

Fred Brizzi gave the picture to the Anglin family, who then kept it secret for almost 25 years. It's a fascinating picture of two men who look to be in their 40's; "Clarence" in the picture is slightly over-weight, and "John" gives the camera a shy smile. Both men wear sunglasses.

"I was there when Fred Brizzi presented the picture to us. It was overwhelming to hear his story, but at the same time we knew so little about him so we were a bit skeptical at first. So many different people have reached out to us over the years, claiming to know where John and Clarence are," David Widner says.

What happened to Frank Morris, Fred Brizzi didn't know – but he did give the family a possible clue:

"According to Brizzi, there was another American living with John and Clarence on the same farm. The man lived there with an American wife, but Brizzi did not know if it was Frank or someone else. It would have been smart for all three to stay together, even after the escape", David Widner says.

The years passed, and the photo was kept secret. Fred Brizzi died in the 1990's, and it would take until 2015 until his photo finally saw the light of day. The reason for this, says Ken Widner, is that John and Clarence were too young in the 90's. If they were alive today they would be 88 and 87 years old, so their family hopes the authorities would be lenient if they were to be caught:

"If we were to find them alive – and there is a small chance that they are still alive – we would ask that they be released for time served. I mean, 53 years!", he says.

A forensic expert that was hired by History Channel reached the conclusion that it was "highly likely" that the picture in Brazil indeed was of John and Clarence Anglin, but lead investigator Michael Dyke is a bit more vary when I e-mail him in October of 2015:

"We'll see, it is a poor-quality photo and not likely to be able to get a good match. They are conveniently wearing sunglasses…"

By the end of 2016 we e-mail again, and by this time Dyke and his colleagues had done a thorough, official analysis of the picture:

"I personally analyzed the Brazil photo and compared it to existing photos of John and Clarence Anglin. I fairly quickly came to the conclusion that neither subject could be one of the Anglin brothers. Due to the poor quality of the Brazil photo, my analysis was based on body type, including arm length, hand length and measurements between clearly defined joints such as the distance between the knuckle and first finger joint. Clarence Anglin had unusually long arms, much longer than the Brazil subject, and John Anglin had much longer hands and fingers than the subject in the Brazil photo. To verify this, the US Marshals Services used an independent, reputable facial recognition expert. He basically confirmed the above listed conclusion, but facial recognition experts rarely, if ever, say anything is a hundred percent yes or no", Dyke writes.

Ken and David Widner are sure, however, that the photograph is genuine. I ask them what they would say to their uncles if they were to find them alive against all odds. The other end of the line suddenly falls silent, while the brothers are thinking. Finally, David Widner laughs out loud:

"I'd just say "Good to see you, boys!""

His big brother Ken is more serious when he answers:

"I have so many questions I would like to ask them. I wouldn't know where to start".

***

Of all the ex-cons I interviewed for this book, Frank Sprenz is the only one who claims to know exactly what happened to the escapees. The others are more cautious in their theories, or they claim to not have an inkling as to what happened to the men:

"Frank Morris and I became sort of friends. His cell was next to mine. I have no idea whether they survived or not, but I certainly hope they did", Rafael Cancel Miranda (1163-AZ) says.

"I heard they found rafts on the other side of the Bay. I think they made it", Jerry Clymore says.

In a letter that he sends from prison in Ohio in February of 2016, Frank Sprenz claims to know exactly what happened to the escapees. According to him, they got help from a powerful prisoner from New York by the name of Bumpy Johnson (1117-AZ):

"Bumpy Johnson told me what happened right after the escape," Sprenz says.

"Johnson and eight of his people were the only negroes on Alcatraz. Bumpy was the crime king of Harlem, and had enormous resources of people and money. He hated what Alcatraz stood for so much that he willingly encouraged the escape and put his people on the outside to help."

According to Frank Sprenz, Bumpy Johnson managed to contact his people, and made sure that Frank Morris and the brothers Anglin were able to escape the country in the days following the escape:

"The escapees were picked up in San Francisco, taken by car to Los Angeles, then by semi-truck to New Orleans where they boarded a freighter headed south," Sprenz says.

Lead investigator Michael Dyke thinks it would be impossible to find the escapees if they managed to get across the southern border:

"Besides the Bumpy Johnson rumors there are other rumors with South America as a reported destination. They are basically all virtually impossible to prove or disprove. Most South American countries have little or no record-keeping to document any such migration of the escapees to the south. If they did have records, they would have either been destroyed by now or lost in the last 50 plus years," he writes me.

"If you consider the possibility of those rumors logically, think about the following information. The prisoners, Bumpy Johnson, and any of the middle men involved, including the person in control of the boat would have little or no knowledge of the exact currents and winds on the night of the escape in order to properly position a boat to intercept three men in a raft, or much less, three men swimming. And it was in the dark. A raft would be affected by both current and winds. The currents were at an ever-increasing speed toward the ocean until a little after midnight on the night of the escape. Also, really? Why would Bumpy Johnson help them? If you consider the items found after the escape in the bay, they were all scattered throughout the bay, because the bay currents are so unpredictable. I would say that it is virtually impossible for a boat to find the three men in the bay in the dark with swift currents having different effects on both of them. Similarly it would be almost impossible for the three men to battle currents and wind to get to the boat," Dyke continues.

Ellsworth "Bumpy" Johnson, 1117-AZ

"It is unlikely that even if they went to South America, that they would never contact any family member or fiancé again. They all had previous escapes and escape attempts and each one, either contacted some friends or relatives after the escape or were apprehended again after."

It has also been speculated that the escapees were helped in a similar manner by another powerful gangster who did time on Alcatraz at the time: Meyer "Mickey" Cohen (1518-AZ), who once was the leader of the Jewish Mafia in Los Angeles.

But Frank Sprenz disputes that theory:

"Mickey Cohen had zero to do with the Anglins and Morris. He didn't have the Bumpy Johnson hatred of Alcatraz. Even his demeanor discounted his desire to embarrass the prison system, for he was a compulsive-obsessive neurotic; washed his hands ten times an hour, carried a roll of toilet paper and used folds of it to insulate his hands from any item someone may hand him," he says.

***

Fifty-six years have passed. So what happened?

Are the remains of the three men on the bottom of the Pacific Ocean, or in an unmarked grave somewhere in the Brazilian countryside? Or are they still living out there in the world – three old men who accomplished the impossible over a half-century ago, and were rewarded with a long life in freedom?

When this book went to print, Frank Morris and the Anglin brothers fate was still unknown. But maybe it doesn't matter if we will never know exactly what happened to them.

Ex-inmate Bill Baker (1259-AZ) doesn't seem to think so, at least. He becomes slightly philosophical when he talks about the three men who vanished way back when the 1960s was in its infancy:

"They did escape, that is a fact. They were alive when they left, so if they died – they died free", he says.

"That is my take on it. They were successful, regardless".

1163-AZ

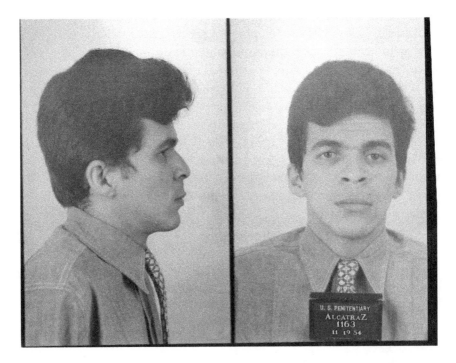

A Latin American woman sits in the visitor gallery of the U.S. House of Representatives, surrounded by three dark-haired men. Silently, the group recites The Lord's prayer and then picks up semi-automatic guns. No one reacts when they point the deadly weapons at the politicians below.

Only when they start shooting, and by then it's too late.

The rain is pouring down over Washington D.C., and inside the giant, dome-shaped Capitol building, smartly dressed congressmen take turns at the podium. It is March 1, 1954, a sleepy afternoon in the House. Only a few people – mostly tourists – sit in the gallery that looks over the large plenary hall.

Grave-looking men, because the 83rd Congress consists of almost only men, discuss immigration this day. The talk is especially centered around Mexico, and how the United States should react to the flow of illegal immigrants that have recently come across the southern border. It is a debate that could be had in 2018, but the year is 1954. A stable and relatively uneventful year, politically speaking: Eisenhower has been president for fourteen months, and the U.S. economy is slowing recovering after a short-term recession in the wake of the costly Korea war.

It's nearly three o'clock when a woman shouts: "¡Viva Puerto Rico libre!"

Suddenly, the calm is replaced by total chaos: shot after shot – thirty, all in all – is fired from the visitor gallery, and those who are hit by the bullets crumple in pain. Five congressmen are injured and lie bleeding on the floor: Alvin Bentley from Michigan is hit in the chest; Clifford Davis from Tennessee in the leg; Ben Jensen from Iowa, George Hyde Fallon from Maryland and Kenneth Roberts from Alabama are all hit in the back.

Four terrorists from Puerto Rico are taken into custody. All of them are eventually sentenced to long prison terms, and the authorities choose to send them to four different institutions.

The youngest terrorist, Rafael Cancel Miranda, draws the shortest straw. He is only 24 years old when he boards a boat that takes him to America's most feared prison.

***

The attack against the Capitol dominated the news in the spring of 1954, and although the five congressmen all recovered from their injuries there were some who argued that the terrorists should be given the death sentence.

That did not happen, but it would be 25 years before President Jimmy Carter decided to pardon and deport them to Puerto Rico in 1979.

Today three of them are dead; Lolita Lebrón died 2010, Andrés Figueroa Cordero in 1979 (of cancer) and Irvin Flores in 1994.

The only one still living is Rafael Cancel Miranda, born July 18, 1930. These days he is a free man residing in his native Puerto Rico, where some view him as a national treasure of sorts due to his life-long struggle for Puerto Rican independence. But his efforts have so far been in vain; Puerto Rico is and remains an "autonomous territory" that belongs to the United States.

Of all the killers, bank robbers and kidnappers that populated Alcatraz, prisoner 1163-AZ stands out as a particularly odd specimen. Rafael was one of very few non-Americans that were sent to the island, and even though he was guilty of a violent crime, his motive was something as unusual as patriotism. Despite this, he seems to have been liked by the other inmates during his time in prison:

"Rafael Miranda is one of the nicest people I've ever met. He was a prince," Harvey Carignan (935-AZ) says.

"Rafael was one of two men who didn't belong on Alcatraz at all. The other one was Morton Sobell (996-AZ). They were political prisoners, not criminals," Bob Schibline (1355-AZ) says.

Sobell – who was an accomplice of the infamous (and later executed) couple Ethel and Julius Rosenberg, and who served time on Alcatraz for helping them spy on the U.S. on behalf of the Soviet Union – became close friends with Rafael on the island. Both men were ideologically driven men with heavily leftist leanings:

"I spoke to him several years ago when I was in New York. I haven't spoken to him since then, but I do have his telephone number," Rafael writes me.

"I will never forget that when he was about to leave Alcatraz, he told me that he wished it were me and not him who was leaving."

We e-mail each other back and forth during the winter of 2016. Rafael responds carefully and seriously to my questions, and he is very helpful: he attaches a scanned, yellowed, Puerto Rican news article from July 1954 in one of his e-mails. Since the text is in Spanish, he has taken the time to translate it into English for me:

Rafael Cancel Miranda, a nationalist convicted in New York and one of the four that fired on Congress last March, boards a ferry on his way to Alcatraz Prison in the San Francisco Bay. Handcuffed and chained to guard Emile Richner, Cancel Miranda was convicted for injuring five congressmen, including representative Alvin M. Bentley, who is currently in San Juan. At Alcatraz, considered one the 'hardest' federal prisons, Cancel Miranda will serve a sentence of 25 to 75 years. When Cancel Miranda boarded the ferry Warden Johnson, he declared to journalists: 'What I did was for the freedom and dignity of my people'.

Miranda's memory is crystal clear, and he sounds proud when he recounts all the years he has spent in prison as a result of his patriotism:

"In 1948, as soon as I reached 18 years of age, the United States government tried to force me to join their army and go to war to kill Koreans. I refused and was sentenced to 2 years in prison in Tallahassee, Florida, USA. I was released in April of 1951. In 1954, I was incarcerated at Alcatraz Prison for 6 years, after which I was transferred to Leavenworth Prison in Kansas, and after 9 years, to Marion Federal Prison in Illinois. Why was I in prison? Because all my life I have been fighting for the freedom of my country," he writes in one of the e-mails.

He doesn't mention the men he shot. It's only when I ask him if he regrets his actions that he talks about his victims. It is as if the five congressmen ceased to be persons of flesh and blood the same moment they became elected by the American people.

Instead, Miranda spontaneously tells of a heroic incident that took place one day in the Alcatraz cell house – when he claims to have saved a prisoner from falling to his death:

"On one occasion, I was living on the second tier of cell blocks and a young prisoner fell from the third floor. I heard the noise, looked up and saw him falling. I stretched my arms and pushed him toward me. A prisoner saw that I had saved the young man's life. A group of them asked the administration that if a prisoner is punished for doing something wrong, why isn't he rewarded when he does something like saving another person's life. The reward requested was to transfer me to another prison, a request that, of course, was not granted"," he writes.

As a dark-haired South American, Rafael ended up in a kind of no-mans-land in the segregated prison. Some of his memories are marred by linguistic misunderstandings:

"I'm smiling remembering an incident that happened in the dining hall at Alcatraz. It was Christmas time and the jailers up put a big Christmas tree in the room. I'm sure they had good intentions, but for the prisoners it brought back memories of better times. So one day, one of the prisoners couldn't stand the sight of the Christmas tree anymore and picked it up and started running with it around the dining hall, the tree falling apart and the guards in pursuit, while the other prisoners cheered and applauded. He was locked up for a while, but he became one of our heroes. I even remember his name: Greenleaser. Needless to say, the prison administration never put up another Christmas tree."

Several other, former prisoners recall the incident during the Christmas holidays in 1959 – both Frank Sprenz (1414-AZ) and James Bulger (1428-AZ) describe the exact same scene in their letters to me – but there was never any prisoner named "Greenleaser" on Alcatraz. The prisoner that massacred the Christmas tree was Homer Clinton (1294-AZ), and his nickname on the island was "The Green Lizard".

***

Homer Clinton, 1294-AZ

"He was called "Green Lizard" after an aftershave of the same name. He used to drink it," Sprenz explains.

It is easy to imagine Rafael Cancel Miranda sitting there in the dining room, in the chaos that ensued. How he turns to the prisoner next to him and asks, in his broken English, what the prisoner who has just attacked the Christmas tree is named.

How he receives the answer "Green Lizard" and, 58 years later, still remembers it as "Greenleaser".

I ask Rafael why he ended up hating the United States. Where did all the animosity come from?

He responds by going back over a hundred years in time, when the U.S. first seized his homeland:

"On May 12, 1898, the United States Army bombed San Juan, Puerto Rico, killing many Puerto Rican civilians in their homes and on the streets of the city. Two months later, on July 25, 1898, the United States invaded my country. Since then we have been a colony of United States imperialism. On more than one occasion, they have massacred my people. My country, Puerto Rico, is in a state of slavery."

What made you decide to attack the US Capitol? I ask him.

"In 1953, the US government tried to deceive the United Nations and the world stating that Puerto Rico had achieved self-government", Rafael responds.

"This was completely false, so on March 1, 1954 Lolita Lebrón, Andrés Figueroa Cordero, Irvin Flores and myself carried out an armed demonstration at the House of Representatives in Washington DC. in order to call the attention of world to unmask the farce being carried out before the international community. The four of us went to trial in Washington DC and New York. Ms. Lebrón was sentenced to 56 years in prison, Figueroa and Flores were sentenced to 81 years and I was sentenced to 84 years (3 extra years for contempt of court). From the courtroom, we were sent to different prisons. I was sent straight to Alcatraz."

Being critical of the U.S. in many regards, do you feel like you were treated differently by the guards or other prisoners?

"During my six years at Alcatraz, I made many friends among the prisoners and no enemies. So much so that sometimes I would take a nap on a bench in the prison yard while the other prisoners were around. At first, it seemed to me that the prisoners couldn't understand the reasons why I did what I did. On one occasion a prisoner asked me how much money I had been paid for participating in the attack on the House of Representatives. When I answered that nobody had to pay me to fight for my people, and that I would pay for the honor, he seemed very surprised. Years later, many of the prisoners seemed to understand."

Since Alcatraz was racially segregated, did you have any problem fitting in?

"I was assigned to live among the white prisoners, although it wouldn't have made any difference to me if I had been assigned to the area for black prisoners. I had friends in both groups, although I well aware of the animosity that existed between the two races.

Once, a white prisoner told me that I was too friendly with the black prisoners. I answered: "Sorry, brother, but I chose my own friends". On one occasion there was an ugly incident in the yard between the white and black prisoners, but I was not there."

Five congressmen were wounded as a result of your armed demonstration. With the passage of time, have you ever felt regret over that fact?

"I wish there was no need for violence, but if it is used against your people, you have the right to fight back by whatever means," Rafael answers.

"On May 12, 1898, United States troops, commanded by admiral Sampson bombarded my country killing civilians in their homes and on the streets of the city of San Juan. Two months later, on July 25, 1898, military forces of the US invaded Puerto Rico and since then my country has been a US colony."

***

Few people go through life free from self-doubt. It seems this would be particularly difficult when you have shot several unarmed people. But Rafael Cancel Miranda will go to his death fully convinced that what he did as an idealistic 23-year-old was completely justified:

"What we did was necessary. I don't regret it and never will. I would rather embrace people than attack them, but if they hurt my people, I will fight back," he writes in an e-mail.

Then he adds:

"It is the United States imperialists who should regret all the crimes they have been committing against humanity. As you know, the list is a very long one."

1339-AZ

What would you do in order to survive? Would you stab a naked, innocent man?

Jerry Clymore asked himself that question in a cell on Alcatraz.

And concluded that there was only one possible answer.

***

A morning in 1960, a black prisoner named James Gilliam (1361-AZ) is in the mess hall serving breakfast to queuing prisoners. He is about to pour some milk to a white prisoner named Joe Wagstaff (1072-AZ) when he suddenly finds himself face-to-face with death.

Whites and blacks had an unspoken agreement on the island. The U.S. was still a highly segregated country at this time, and that was also true of its most infamous prison:

"There were only ten blacks on the island; Bumpy Johnson (1117-AZ) and his crew. They were segregated on B-block, west side, first floor, first ten cells from the back end. They even went into the dining room as the only group. "The Rock" had strict segregation," Frank Sprenz (1414-AZ) writes in a letter.

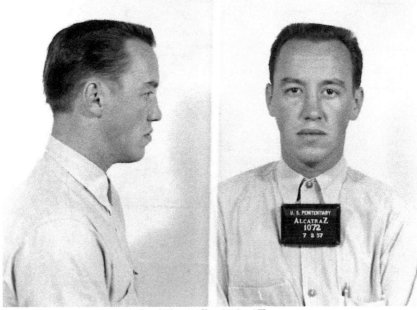

Joe Wagstaff, 1072-AZ

"The only time they were around whites was yard time, and then they grouped together on the large steps with Bumpy on the top step presiding. If you had trouble with one of them, you had major problems with all of them. I've never heard of anyone ignorant enough to stab one of them for it was a guaranteed death sentence," Sprenz continues.

But James Gilliam was an unusually disliked prisoner – by black and white inmates alike:

"He infuriated the convicts by talking about how when he got free, he would rape all of our wives and children – incendiary talk – and all locked down, no one could get at him. Later, some people drew straws, and Wagstaff drew the shortest one," James "Whitey" Bulger (1428-AZ) writes.

"So he stabbed Gilliam in the chest in the mess hall, but the knife hit bone and didn't penetrate deep enough. A guard, Bill Long, grabbed Joe's wrist with both hands. Then he noticed the knife and held on for dear life."

James Gilliam was rushed to the prison hospital, where his wounds were treated. He returned to the general prison population after a short convalescence. Wagstaff was thrown in the "Hole" in D-block, and the dramatic episode appeared to be over.

But it wasn't.

***

I call Jerry Clymore 58 years after he arrived on Alcatraz as prisoner number 1339-AZ. These days, he is a deeply religious man living a quiet life with his wife in Washington State, but back then – in June of 1958 – he was a boisterous, 24-year-old bank robber who had been trouble in every prison he had ever been in:

"I did a bank robbery and they sent me to federal institution. I think it was in Indiana somewhere. I didn't last very long there, because I wasn't easily pushed around. On the first day they gave me a pair of pants that were too long for me, so I rolled them up. I started down the hall, and one of the guards said: "Hey, roll them pants down!". I told him: "You want them pants down, you roll them down. I'm not rolling them down". That took me to my first trip to "The Hole"…"

Jerry is a friendly man who sounds significantly younger than his 82 years, and he is short of breath when he comes to the phone on a summer evening in 2016:

"You caught me right in a mess here. One of the boards on our fence had come loose, and we have little kids and dogs in the backyard…", he says with a little laugh.

Jerry has first informed me that he wants all communication between us to be done via e-mail, and that he prefers to leave his past behind him:

"I had received two letters from the persons that I believe to be in charge of what Alcatraz has become, with similar requests. That was six or seven years ago. I failed to answer them. Your letter touched me differently. I feel like I should respond. It has caused me to think back at those years," he writes in an e-mail.

When I ask if we can talk a little bit about his childhood, he changes his mind and agrees to talk on the phone. And as soon as I call him, he goes straight to the heart of the matter:

"I've been trying to figure out what motivated me, what caused me to turn towards crime. The simplest way I can I explain it is I just didn't seem to fit in, you know? I couldn't run fast enough or jump high enough, or have enough strength to be good in sports. I wasn't a really talkative person, but pretty shy," he says.

As a kid Jerry took an interest in larger-than-life gangsters like Al Capone and George "Machine Gun" Kelly.

"I grew up under pretty stressful circumstances for the country. The Prohibition…all that did was create an enormous criminal organization. The press wrote a lot of stories that kind of glamorized the crooks and the bank robbers when I grew up. That may have played a part for me," later on.

Jerry Wayne Clymore was born on June 10, 1934. During his early childhood, the Clymore family – Jerry, his father Noel, mother Mary and little brother Ray – moved from state to state:

"I was born in Oklahoma. My mother was part Cherokee Indian, and the people in Oklahoma are very prejudiced against Indians, like they are against Mexicans and blacks. They wouldn't do anything out front, but it was there," he says.

"When I was seven or eight we moved to Long Beach in California, and my dad went to work on the shipyards there. World War II started around that time, but he got a deferment because he had two small kids and worked in a shipyard," Jerry continues.

He describes his father as being a man who both worked and drank hard. During the 1940's, Noel Clymore took on one low-paid job after another, and his family had no choice but to follow him wherever he moved:

"My father provided fairly well for us. He was very loyal to his family. He had his short-comings, but he was never neglectful and he never abused my mother in anyway. He was a drinker, but he was one of those weekend drinkers. Friday night after work, you know, that was when he'd bring out the bottle."

Soon after the end of World War II it was time for the family to move again:

"We moved to a little town in Texas when I was 10 or 11, and my dad worked in the oil fields. There was a lot of racism against Mexicans there, and I really resented that. They were so prejudiced against Mexicans in that town – the Mexicans couldn't even go to the movies, except for Saturdays. And then they had to go in through the back door and sit on the balcony," Jerry remembers.

"One of my best friends was a Mexican; his mother used to give me little treats and stuff. I really loved that lady. It upset me to see her people being treated like that. I never acted out on it, but I never liked it."

In his teens, Jerry began to experiment with drugs, which he thinks may be the biggest reason why he later started robbing banks. He simply needed to pay for what gradually developed into an addiction:

"I think I went into crime because of drugs. That, and just not fitting in anywhere," he says.

After getting busted for a bank robbery in Louisiana he was sentenced to prison, where he soon got into trouble for being rude to the guards. The rolled-up-pants incident was just the first of many run-ins with the authorities:

"I had a couple of similar episodes, and they sent me to Leavenworth. There we decided we'd have a food strike, because the food wasn't no good. As one of the leaders in that incident they decided to send me to Alcatraz."

Most of the men who got sent to "The Rock" remember being scared when they first arrived. But Jerry claims that he was pretty relaxed about doing time there:

"Actually, it wasn't scary. Not to me, anyway. There were people there that I knew. I had a friend there who introduced me to people. A bit like "You bother him, you bother me. I got a free ride through the place," he says.

In the beginning, Jerry became known as something of a pacifist among the other prisoners, James "Whitey" Bulger remembers:

"Jerry and I worked in the clothing room by the shower room. Jerry read a lot, and I remember him discussing (Mahatma) Gandhi's philosophy of "Ahimsa", non-violent resistance. I told him that would never work on 'The Rock'."

On Alcatraz, it was necessary for a young and small-statured guy like Jerry to have friends. Otherwise, he ran the risk of becoming prey for older, tougher cons who wanted a gay lover – a "punk", in prison slang - to rule over:

"I didn't have any trouble getting along with people. It seems I was blessed that way. Maybe some people wanted to make a punk out of me, but that didn't happen," he says.

But it soon became apparent that the friendships he enjoyed on the island came with a price. In early 1960, Jerry learned that one of his friends was in trouble:

"Another prisoner, who was a good friend, sent word to me. He was in isolation and said he believed he was in danger when he got out. He asked me to take care of it," he remembers.

To "take care of it" could mean only one thing; Jerry was told to hurt – preferably kill – a complete stranger. The man was James Gilliam (1361-AZ), a 30-year-old robber and burglar from Alabama who had arrived at Alcatraz on July 11, 1958. Gilliam was doing his second stint on the island; in 1951 he was sent there to serve another term as prisoner 932-AZ.

For some reason, Gilliam had threatened to kill Jerrys' friend as soon as he would get out of isolation. Instead of taking care of the threat himself, his friend wanted Jerry to get rid of James Gilliam.

Jerry was suddenly faced with a terrible dilemma. He was not a violent man by nature, yet he would have to commit a vicious assault – which would very likely result in a man losing his life.

There was also the risk that Jerry himself would be killed or seriously injured, because the man he was about to attack was much bigger and stronger than himself:

"Gilliam was strong and weighed about 265 lbs., Jerry weighed maybe 140 or 145," writes James "Whitey" Bulger.

Jerry claims that he didn't really have a choice in the matter:

"It was part of the prison "code" and you lived by that code or you were an outcast whose life was in danger," he says.

Still, I persist, you must have had some doubts about what you were asked to do?

"No, I was just tuned up that way. It didn't seem to be anything more than "this has got to happen," you know", Jerry answers.

***

During the summer of 1960, Jerry prepared for his attack on James Gilliam:

"I chose to do it in the shower room, because that's the most vulnerable place. I don't remember who I got the knife from, it was always available if you needed one," he says.

"Whitey" Bulger, who worked with Jerry in the clothing room, witnessed the attack – which took place on August 27, 1960 – up close:

"I was three feet away. Jerry stabbed Gilliam deep in the back between the vertebrae. Gilliam hollered, and then Jerry tried to pull the knife out for another go but he couldn't get it out. So Jerry kicked Gilliam in the head, and then a guard jumped on top of him," Bulger writes.

"A new guard stood there looking at Gilliam, who was moaning on the floor. Some cons who were friends of Jerry told the guard: "Pull the knife out!", and the guard did. Blood squirted out, and Gilliam screamed," Bulger continues.

Gilliam barely survived the brutal assault, and was transferred from Alcatraz a few months later. Jerry doesn't want to go into detail about what he remembers of the stabbing, but he briefly notes that his "action assured" his "standing" in the prison.

His friend never personally thanked him for what Jerry had done:

"No, I never saw my friend again. He went to Atlanta before I was released. I'm sure he was thankful," Jerry says.

***

A black prisoner had just been brutally stabbed, but ironically enough it was "Bumpy" Johnson – the most powerful black inmate on Alcatraz – who came to the rescue of Jerry Clymore. When Jerry was charged for the attempted assassination of James Gilliam, the mighty boss of the black mafia in Harlem testified to Jerry's advantage during the trial in San Francisco.

James Gilliam, 1361-AZ

"Bumpy Johnson liked me, he was a friend of mine. He went in there and testified that what I did was what I had to do. After that they found me not guilty," Jerry Clymore says.

Why Bumpy Johnson chose to help a white prisoner like this seems inexplicable; maybe James Gilliam had done something to offend him, too. Gilliam certainly seems to have been an unpopular convict:

"We all volunteered to be witnesses for Jerry. He went to the 'Hole' afterwards, and I never saw him again. So much for *Ahimsa* and Mahatma Ghandi!," "Whitey" Bulger writes.

Jerry emphasizes that he never had a racist motive for assaulting Gilliam; something that has incorrectly been reported throughout the years:

"No, that wasn't what it was about. I could see why someone would think that, but Bumpy Johnson was probably the most influential black in the prison system and he was friend of mine. And he went to testify for me," he says.

Jerry Clymore, circa 1960

James Gilliam was transferred to the Medical Center in Springfield, Missouri:

"He was taken off the island on a stretcher – screwed up and his sex life over – all thoughts of rape now just a dream," James "Whitey" Bulger writes with ill-concealed glee.

***

After the trial was concluded, Jerry Clymore was sent back to Alcatraz. A jury had just acquitted him of the assault, but Alcatraz had laws of its own. The guards who had seen the incident were convinced that it was not a matter of self-defense – and that Jerry should be punished for stabbing Gilliam:

"I'm amazed at the jury's action. I just don't believe it was self-defense. Regardless pf the acquittal, Clymore will go back to solitary confinement because the prison disciplinary board has already held him responsible for the stabbing," Warden Paul Madigan told the *San Francisco Chronicle*.

Jerry was moved to isolation in D-block, where he remained until his transfer from Alcatraz in January 1963. Initially he was locked up in one of the dark strip cells. As previously noted, an inmate could only be placed in the dreaded "Hole" for a period of nineteen days, but Jerry claims that he was in there for far longer than that:

"I was in there for ninety days. I was in a cell with no bed or no mattress, they wouldn't even give us a blanket sometimes. You just sat there in the dark for 24 hours. They fed you bread and water. They didn't use any violence on Alcatraz, like they did in some of the state prisons. This was another form of extreme punishment," Jerry says.

He describes the rest of his time in D-block as being incredibly boring. Unlike the other prisoners on Alcatraz, those who were locked up in isolation were not allowed to leave their cells other than to shower and visit the yard once a week. All meals were taken in their cells. After a few years of this monotonous routine, Jerry and some other prisoners decided to carry out a dramatic protest action:

"Six of us had razor blades smuggled in, and we cut our heel straps to protest against the system. It really hurt, but I didn't sever them completely so it healed itself. And it had no effect, they just patched us up and then it was back to the cell and the same old, same old," he says.

***

Jerry was transferred from Alcatraz in 1963. He was first sent back to Leavenworth, and during the next twenty years he was moved around from prison to prison: San Quentin, McNeil Island, Monroe in Washington State, while slowly developing a heroin addiction. The few times he was released back into society, he almost immediately committed a new crime to support his addiction and was returned to prison.

It was a deadly spiral that seemed to have no end, but in the late 1970's, Jerry experienced something that turned his life around:

"In 1979 I was convicted of robbery while I was in a Spokane, Washington county jail. I woke up in my cell as an inner voice spoke to me saying, "Jerry. Say the Lord's Prayer". I did and what happened is nothing shy of a miracle. I became a different person. The change was gradual. I became a different person. I now have 31 years in Alcoholics Anonymous. I'm a member of Crossover Church, and thanks to God and Jesus I have a full and peaceful life," he says.

Jerry and Peg Clymore, 2006

When Jerry was let free for good – in 1985 – he did some volunteer work in a Spokane church, working with criminals and trying to "help them discover ways to change their lives". In the late 1980's, he fell in love with a woman named Peg:

"In '91 I was married and in '92 we moved to Walsenburg, Colorado, to be near her folks. I got a job painting houses. These years have been full and wonderful. Health and age have brought us back to Spokane. I read and sometimes play with my grandkids. They are six and three, and that's a job in itself..."

The children are actually the grandkids of Jerry's wife; he never had any biological children himself, but he takes the role of stepfather and step-grandfather seriously.

He has lived a long and rich life, and he sounds happy when we talk. Still, I get the feeling that Jerry has chosen to repress a lot of the memories from his decades in the toughest prisons in the United States – especially the day when he stabbed a helpless man in the shower room on Alcatraz. It's clear he doesn't like to talk about it; nevertheless, I ask him carefully if he feels sad, thinking back on the incident today.

"Oh yeah," Jerry answers.

"The guy didn't deserve it. But on the other hand, somebody was gonna get hurt. Me, my friend, or somebody."

1355-AZ

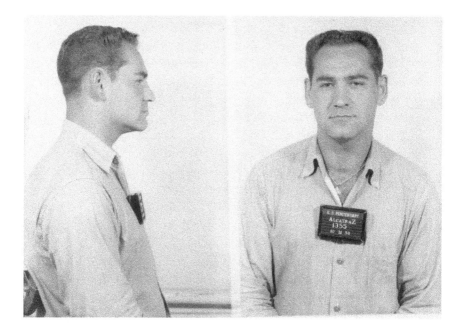

Robert Schibline is 26 and scared to death.

The 6'3" former U.S. Navy diver stands on Fisherman's Wharf and stares at the menacing looking island that will be his home for many years to come. "Bob" is street smart, a good fighter who is accustomed to the ways of prison.

But Alcatraz is not your average prison.

"You had been hearing stories your whole life, about what kind of animals were inside of there. So naturally you were apprehensive" he says over the phone from Lake Wales, Florida.

"I had a reputation of being an enforcer. But when I looked at Alcatraz, I thought, 'My God, there must be 250 people out there, and every one of them probably thinks *he* is the enforcer'."

When Bob Schibline arrived in June 1958, Alcatraz was in many ways a different prison compared to the one that had welcomed Al Capone and his mafia buddies back in the 30's. Almost no glamorous "public enemies" were left on the island (only Alvin Karpis, and Bob made sure to seek him out in the yard one day). Capone was a distant memory; as were Machine Gun Kelly and Doc Barker. In their place, the cells were mostly populated by poor, small-time criminals who had grown up during the Depression.

In 1958, you no longer had to be notorious to get sent to Alcatraz. To be violent and desperate was plenty enough.

Bob Schibline was a young man who fit the template perfectly. He was born August 23, 1931, in Winnebago County, Wisconsin, and endured a childhood that was both tough and tragic:

"My father died when I was five and my mother when I was six or seven. My brother and sister were from a previous marriage. and were sent off to their kin. I don't know what relation my kin were to me, but we lived in a one room shack that had blankets hung to divide the house into four rooms. The toilet was an outhouse. I lasted about a year, and then was passed on to someone else," he says.

He is not the type who wants to delve into the past, or think too deeply about how his childhood affected him:

"Really not much to talk about, but I grew-up hard," he says.

Bob enlisted in the Navy at 20 years old, but soon got bored with the rules and regulations and started robbing banks on his spare time. He says he found it to be exciting – but that wasn't the only reason:

"It was exciting, sure. But when I was in the Navy we were getting paid thirty dollars a month, which wasn't a lot of money. The banks, however, had a lot of money."

During their permissions, Bob and a Navy friend became partners in crime. Armed with two guns (one in each hand) they proceeded to the nearest bank office and demanded money. Then they hurried back to *USS Franklin D. Roosevelt* where they were stationed – the huge war ship was a "getaway car" as good as any:

"The banks were easy to rob back then, they didn't have a bunch of cameras like they do today. I knocked off six banks when I was in the Navy", Bob says.

Bob and his friend eventually got caught, however, and Bob was sent to the Leavenworth prison in Kansas on a five-year sentence.

But he wasn't to spend a lot of time there:

"I was a rebel, and I was very well trained in martial arts. I had no fear of any one person. We had a small uprising at Leavenworth, and I was picked up as one of the ringleaders. Together with 23 others I was shipped to the Rock," Bob says.

"The cons I found on the Rock were a very tight group; names, money, or titles meant nothing. As a rule you had to be on the Rock long enough for the ink on your number to be very dry before they would acknowledge your presence there. Somehow, they found out I was a scuba diver – this was a new thing back then – so I was welcomed into the fold.

Bob describes the daily routine on the island as deadly boring:

"We had no newspapers, no news magazines, no news on the radio. We had two earphone jacks in our cell; one for sports and the other for radio shows like Matt Dillon. Our news source was from new inmates coming in," he says.

"Rehabilitation meant nothing, Alcatraz was meant to break us, physically, in sprit, mentally and morally."

Getting out of his cell to work during the days cured some of the boredom and loneliness he felt, however briefly. Bob Schibline worked three different jobs during his five years on the island:

"My first job was a pattern cutter in the clothing factory, for the men who ran the sewing machines to make white baker and cook uniforms that were sent to other federal prisons."

"On my second job, I was assigned to the labor gang to do construction work around Alcatraz. One thing we did was build a fuel oil storage tank with cement in an area next to the island power plant. We jack hammered down in bedrock about 5 feet, and built walls above-ground about 5 feet, so we had 40 feet by 40 feet by 10 feet room. I loved this kind of work."

His time on the labor gang almost ended in disaster for Bob, however:

"I almost got shot on the job. It was hard work, hauling wet cement in wheel barrows, and I had my shirt off a lot. I used to hang it on a fence. Then, one day, they came to get us at noon for dinner in a pickup truck. I was halfway to the truck when I remembered my shirt. I spun around and ran towards my shirt, when a shot rang out from the guard in the guard tower on top of the old industries building. I stopped short and pointed to my shirt. Got the o.k. and lived to eat dinner. Talk about trigger happy guards!"

Allen "Geno" Scusselle, 1356-AZ

His third and final job on Alcatraz was on the dock, where Bob worked as a heavy equipment operator and later as a mechanic. It was, however, on the labor gang where he felt most at home:

"I really liked that labor gang, because it kept me from getting soft. I worked with my buddy Geno Scusselle (1356-AZ), We were handcuffed together from Leavenworth. He came up to me there and asked if I would teach him martial arts. I did, and we got busted together and came to The Rock together. I really liked him, but the died some years ago."

***

Alcatraz did not rehabilitate Bob Schibline. On the contrary, he was determined to continue robbing banks as soon as he was released. Therefore, he sought out two of America's most notorious criminals to ask them for their advice.

One of them was Alvin "Creepy" Karpis (325-AZ), who had been on the island since 1936. Karpis was one of only four men to be appointed Public Enemy #1 by J. Edgar Hoover's FBI (the other three were John Dillinger, Charles "Pretty Boy" Floyd and George "Baby Face" Nelson). This dubious honor had been bestowed upon him after a series of bank robberies and a widely publicized 1933 kidnapping of millionaire William Hamm in Minnesota.

Alvin Karpis, 325-AZ

In early 1958 - after 22 years on Alcatraz - Karpis was temporarily transferred to Leavenworth, where Bob Schibline was incarcerated at the time:

"But after six months he got sent back to Alcatraz, on the same chain gang that I was on," Bob remembers.

"Karpis had his fingerprints removed, and I figured if I could do that I could become a new person. So I went up to him one day on the yard and asked him about it. He said, "Well, I used acid, but I don't recommend that because it hurt like hell."

Instead, Karpis urged Bob to go see another famous criminal that resided on the island at the time. Mickey Cohen (1518-AZ) was a long-time boss of the Jewish mafia in Los Angeles, and a former associate of famed mobster Benjamin "Bugsy" Siegel.

"Karpis said 'go see Mickey Cohen about it.' So I went up to Mickey and said, 'hey Mickey, I got a question for you.' And Mickey says, 'who do you need killed?'", Bob remembers with a laugh.

"He gave me the number for a plastic surgeon in Hollywood. He said, "it's gonna cost you. It's gonna be two or three times the normal rate for a plastic surgeon." I replied: "The banks will take care of that."

Meyer "Mickey" Cohen, 1518-AZ

***

When Bob Schibline left Alcatraz in 1963, he had no intention of going straight. But circumstances beyond his control – or fate, if you will – made him turn away from a life of crime.

"I was supposed to meet up with a guy and start robbing banks again. But he got busted before I got out. So I opened up a dive shop instead, and went into business. And the dive shop made more money than the bank robberies, so I just went straight more or less," he says.

Bob Schibline never called the Hollywood surgeon that Mickey Cohen told him about. Instead he got married, and moved to Florida during his later years.

It has been over half a century since he left The Rock behind. But he still hates the former guards on Alcatraz with an intensity that borders on the bizarre. One day I ask him where all his anger stems from:

"Talking to the guards was not done, they treated us like animals in a cage. We were never beaten or anything like that, it was small stuff, like snide remarks. Once I was in the Hole, and one guard would not miss a day without blowing cigarette smoke into my cell. I was without food, but I was always reminded what a cigarette smelled like," Bob says.

"The guards showed their dislike for us with their attitude and manner. They may have forgot about our dislike toward one another, but I have not nor ever will," he continues.

To forgive may be a virtue, and it is said that time heals all wounds. But Robert James Schibline doesn't give a damn about that:

"Every time I hear about another guard dying I get out my cognac and have a little celebration of my own. I know of only four or five guards that are left, so I have plenty of cognac left. But if I run out, I know where I can get more."

Bob in front of his old cell on Alcatraz, 2005. Next to him is his wife Karen and daughter Kelly

1428-AZ

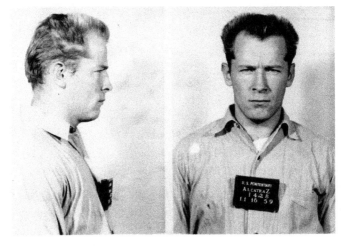

On the evening of May 1, 2011, President Barack Obama went on live tv to report that U.S. forces had killed al-Qaeda leader Osama bin Laden.

Bin Laden had been the most wanted man in America for twelve years; officially since June 7, 1999, when he was promoted to number one on the FBI's "Ten Most Wanted" list. The same moment the terrorist leader was shot dead in his hideaway in Abbottabad, Pakistan, a completely different criminal became the country's most sought-after fugitive.

For 16 years, James "Whitey" Bulger had been on the run from justice. But now the authorities were closing in on the brutal former boss of the Irish mafia in Boston; a man who, for decades, had ruled an entire city with an iron fist and was suspected of having murdered at least 19 people. The FBI announced a reward of $2 million for information that could lead to his arrest, and after barely two months – on June 22, 2011 – an anonymous tip resulted in the 81-year-old Bulger being arrested in Santa Monica, California, together with his girlfriend Catherine.

Five and a half years later, a thick letter arrives in my mailbox. 18 handwritten pages, mailed from a high-security prison in Coleman, Florida, where Bulger is serving a double life sentence as prisoner 02182-748. But he doesn't sign his letter with that number, but rather with another – much older – prison number that he unexpectedly seems to remember with warmth and nostalgia: 1428AZ.

James "Whitey" Bulger will go into history as one of America's most infamous and ruthless criminals. In the books and movies that have been made about him, he is portrayed as a brutal, murderous psychopath. But the letter revolves around three persons who seem to have done the seemingly impossible: touch his hardened heart.

***

September 1988.

James Bulger receives a phone call in Boston. He has just turned 59, and is on the absolute peak of his criminal career. As leader of the so-called Winter/Hill gang, he is control of an enormous, criminal empire involving illegal gambling, money laundering, drug trafficking, extortion – and murder. Bulger rose to the top of the gang in 1979, when many of the Winter/Hill gang's original leaders were arrested and sentenced to prison. He was a man who was, for all practical purposes, above the law, thanks to his close friendship with one of most powerful FBI agents in the city.

During a time when many other mafia leaders could be caught thanks to the U.S. government's tough RICO laws, Bulger was protected by the agent John Connolly who claimed Bulger was an FBI informant (something Bulger denies to this day) – thus needing protection.

The man who answered the phone that day was worth several million dollars. He was a feared person – suspected of having committed many cold-blooded murders over the years – but he was also admired by many in the poor South Boston area where he had grown up. There he was seen as a kind of mythological figure; a contemporary Robin Hood who donated a lot of money to local charities.

The man who called him was another former Alcatraz prisoner, Clarence "Joe" Carnes (714-AZ). Bulger and Carnes served time together on "The Rock" back in the early 60's, and had become close friends through the years.

But now Carnes called with some bad news:

He called me from the Springfield, Mo. prison hospital. He explained: "Since I was 17 years old I've been in prison, and I hate the rules. But then I was paid 35 000 dollars in cash for a movie about my life and said 'to hell with the rules'. I went to San Diego for 'wine, women and song', and thought the money would last forever. Woke up on a park bench, sick, sober and broke. Wound up here."

He told me he would be released Oct. 15, 1988. I told him I would be there to pick him up, with my girlfriend in a limo. Sadly, he took a piece of butter off the food cart a few days later. He was on a diet, and a nurse wrote him up. He lost 30 days of good time, and he called me with the bad news. I said, "Joe, after all these years…but you can handle this. I will be there when you get out. Get the Sunday paper, look for the car ads, pick any one out and I'll buy it for you."

He said, "I'm not sure I can drive." I told him, "I'll send you to driving school."

Days later, I'm having dinner. On the news, they suddenly said, "Famous Alcatraz convict, Joe "The Choctaw Kid" Carnes, dies in prison."

Damn, I thought. For a tab of butter he died behind bars.

When Bulger arrived on Alcatraz in 1959, Clarence "Joe" Carnes had already been there for 14 years. Carnes had been only 18 years old when he got sent to "The Rock", which made him the youngest prisoner ever sent to the island. At age 16, he had killed a man during a robbery of a gas station in Oklahoma, and was sentenced to life imprisonment for murder.

Less than a year after he arrived on Alcatraz, Carnes played a role in the tragedy that came to be known as "The Battle of Alcatraz". Three of his friends were killed, and two were later executed for their roles in the failed escape attempt, which cost two guards their lives.

Carnes himself avoided the death penalty because of the compassion he had shown to guards that had been taken hostage and locked in two cells by the escapees. When it was clear that the escape was doomed to fail, prisoner Joe Cretzer shot the guards one by one in the cells. But not one of his victims was to die instantly (although one guard, William Miller, would die of his wounds many hours later).

When Cretzer realized that the guards he had shot were still alive inside the two cells, he ordered the young and inexperienced Carnes to finish the job:

Cretzer ordered him to cut the throats of the guards. Carnes had a long, carved knife and reached down into the cell. The only guard who ever said a kind word to him had been shot. He said, "Joe, please. I have a wife and children." Joe said he couldn't go through with it. So he rubbed blood on all their throats, and said, "If you move, Joe Cretzer will finish you off."

Carnes was sentenced to 199 years and seven years in isolation in D-block. It aged him. Some convicts later thought he should have cut the guards' throats. But his friends – and I was one of them – felt it was his decision. And it kept him alive. Nothing would have been gained by killing the guards, all had wives and children.

Clarence Carnes was nicknamed "The Choctaw Kid", due to the fact that he was a full-blooded Choctaw Indian. This gave Bulger an idea, when he saw Carnes' obituary in the paper.

Joe was buried in a prison cemetery, so I got in touch with his niece. Long story short, I got an undertaker to exhume Joe, and bought an expensive casket. Then I had Joe taken by hearse, not train, to a cemetery in Oklahoma and set up a funeral there. Had a Choctaw Indian preacher for the ceremony, and Indian women singing. No media vultures, and no white people. Only people from his tribe. He was buried in Billy Cemetery, a Choctaw cemetery in Daisy, Oklahoma. I got a stone with his name: "Clarence Joe Carnes – d.o.b. 1927, died 1988". When I saw the stone for the first time, I realized Joe was only two years older than me. On the Rock I thought of him as an old man.

Bulger is obviously a complicated person, which the generous gesture towards Carnes shows. He is a convicted murderer, but throughout his life he has also been exceedingly loyal to his closest friends:

"Say what you want about 'Whitey'", Charlie Hopkins (1186-AZ) says.

"But he takes care of his real friends."

***

James Joseph Bulger Jr. was born on Sep. 3, 1929, and grew up in a large Irish-American family in a poor community known as South Boston – or "Southie" – in Boston, Massachusetts.

"The South Boston Whitey grew up in was very working class and because the Irish were the dominant ethnic group, it had a very Irish ethos and culture," says Kevin Cullen, a former columnist at the Boston Globe and co-author of Whitey Bulger: America's most wanted gangster and the manhunt that brought him to justice.

"Southie is a peninsula, at one time in the mid-19th century an island connected to the rest of the city by bridges, and that physical insularity bred a psychological insularity. Outsiders were blamed for all that was bad, and there was a tendency to believe the neighborhood was better than others, in part because it did have such physical beauty with the ocean, in part because people in Southie didn't spend much time in other neighborhoods."

One of Bulger's brothers – William, or "Billy" – grew up to become a successful politician who served as President of the Massachusetts Senate for 18 years. By contrast, the young Jimmy turned out to be the black sheep of the family. Already at the age of 13, he had achieved notoriety in the neighborhood as a fierce street fighter and a car thief. He was nicknamed "Whitey" by local policemen, because of his blonde hair.

"Billy and Whitey were similar in many ways, at least in their determination. The biggest difference was Billy succeeded in school and Whitey did not. From talking to people who knew Whitey when he was a kid, and looking at school records, I would bet that Whitey had attention deficit and hyperactivity disorder. Today, he would have been medicated. Back then, he couldn't sit still, was a real distraction in the classroom and was punished as a result. He just seemed to have given up in school. Quit in 9th grade. Billy, on the other hand, did very well in school and saw education as a way out of poverty. He pursued that very diligently. Whitey started looking for more action in his teens. That said, Whitey is a sociopath, and maybe he always was. He could have succeeded in school and still be a sociopath who killed without conscience," Kevin Cullen says.

In the early 1950's, Bulger robbed several banks in Massachusetts, Rhode Island and Indiana. He was arrested in the town of Revere, Massachusetts, in 1956, and was later sentenced to 20 years in prison. He started serving this sentence at the federal prison in Atlanta, Georgia, and soon got involved in an escape attempt.

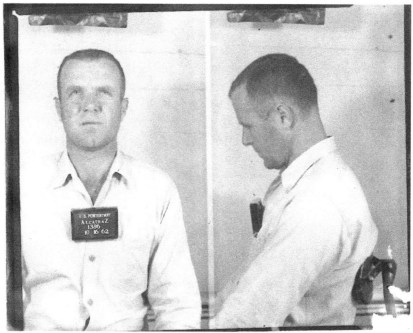

Louis Arquilla, 1386-AZ

The escape failed and was the reason Bulger – along with Louis Arquilla (1386-AZ), Walter Splitt (1408-AZ), John Paul Scott (1403-AZ), John Malone (1401-AZ) and Charlie Catalano (1381-AZ) – got sent to Alcatraz. The incident (and its aftermath, when Bulger almost died in an isolation cell after being subjected to a medical experiment) shows that Atlanta could be just as tough a prison as Alcatraz.

I bribed a guard, and he brought in two blades. Catalano, Arquilla, Scott, Splitt and Maloney checked into the hospital. There they cut out a window, and put a ladder together. But the ladder broke, so they climbed onto the roof and were trapped. The warden told them, "Come down, or we shoot!" They said, "Ok, but first let us finish what will be our last cigarette for a while."

Another prisoner from Ohio, Darby, tock the hacksaw blades to the warden. He said, "Give me a parole, and I'll tell you who else was there. The warden agreed, and Darby said "Bulger". The warden brought me in and said, "I want the name of the guard who brought the blades in. You will tell me now, and save yourself a lot of misery and pain." I told him I didn't know what he was talking about. "Throw him in the Hole!" the warden said.

Hours before I had joined a medical project. It searched for a vaccine for whopping cough, which was the No. 1 killer of infants in the U.S. They shot me up with a big syringe, full of raw whopping cough germs. I had a reaction to it, it felt like I was full of molten lava. My temperature soared, and it felt like my whole body was on fire. A guard called for the doctor. They put me in the hospital, and there they put wet clothes on me to bring down the fever. But when the warden heard I was in the hospital, he said, "He stays in the Hole!"

So I went back to the Hole. The guard who had given the blades to me came into my cell and whispered into my ear. "If you talk about it, they'll put me in here with you." I told him, "Never come near me again. I have forgotten everything." He squeezed my arm: "Thanks."

I spent months in the Hole. It was cold, dark, I was sick and the food was bad. Every now and then they would ask me if I was ready to talk. I told them, "I'm not able to tell you what I don't know."

One morning they told me, "You're going to The Rock." Warden Wilkinson – we called him "Friendly Fred" – was a former Marine who was wounded in the Battle of Iwo Jima. He said, "I should have sent you to Alcatraz right away." I said, "I wish you had!" They thought it was a bad punishment, but Alcatraz was the best prison I did time in. They had the best food, and there I had the only job I ever enjoyed going to.

The 30-year old James Bulger arrived on Alcatraz on November 13, 1959. He was booked as prisoner 1428-AZ.

My first job on The Rock was in the clothing room. Jim Long[3] was the guard in charge of the six of us – Jerry Clymore (1339-AZ), Red McCraw (1406-AZ), Frank Coppola (1368-AZ), Doc Riley (1378-AZ), Johnson (1347-AZ), and me. Jim Long was a young, big guy who was in good physical condition. He was a bit of a bully. Johnson was upset because Long had been too rough handling Homer Clinton (1294-AZ), AKA "Green Lizard", when he attacked the Christmas tree in the mess hall in 1959. Long leaped on Lizard and nearly broke his arm before they dragged him off to the Hole – he was in a rage.

So Johnson didn't like him. Long had a habit of taking off his uniform jacket and draping it on the back of a wooden chair. One day, we finished our work and Long put his jacket on. Suddenly he got real quiet – the left sleeve had been cut off and fell on the floor! Long was speechless. Then he exploded: "I'll kill the M F who did this!"

Red McCraw says, "I didn't do that!" I said to him, "Why did you say that? "Well, I didn't do it." "So what, now you have it down to five? Keep your mouth shut and let him figure it out!"

Long glared at us. Then Johnson says, "Why would anyone do that to you, Long?" He was an older con, a real cool customer. Long got confused. Johnson says, "Maybe it's because you almost broke Homer's arm? And now you're in trouble, having to write that report. You don't know what you want - be liked, or hated."

By now, Long was furious. He looked like an insane man, good thing he wasn't armed. He hollered: "Ok, back to your cells!" Then he puts his hat on, screams and starts shaking his head. A dead mouse was in his hat!

After the torment Bulger and his cohorts put the poor guard through, the prison authorities decided to transfer Bulger to one of the least sought-after workplaces on the island. But this proved to be a lucky break. The time he spent working in the laundry at Alcatraz was to be a surprisingly happy period.

The crew that worked in the laundry were all men who didn't conform to the

---

[3] There is no record of a guard with this name having worked on Alcatraz. Bulger either uses a pseudonym, or misremembers the name.

rules. It was located as close to the water's edge as you could get. We were only separated by a double chain-link fence with barbed wire. Above us was a guard tower, manned by a guard with a .45-caliber pistol and a 1903, bolt action .30-06-caliber Springfield rifle.

The foreman in the laundry was a small, wiry guard in his late fifties. His name was Alver Gustav Bloomquist – he was Swedish. A quiet, gentle guy, married with children, who spoke quietly to the men. Some of the cons were sullen, angry and hateful. But "Bloomie" would greet you, and then say, "I'll show you how to do your job!" He would show you your job, and then ease away. Other guards would stand by and criticize the cons when they made mistakes, but Bloomie would quietly come back and slowly do the work, saying nothing. After a while, the laundry moved along, smooth, like a Swiss watch. Bloomie was like an animal trainer at the circus.

Bloomie smoked cigarettes and was always pleasant and courteous to the men. We would come to work in the AM and slowly got faster at doing the day's work. After a while we could do it all in the AM and Bloomie would let us have the afternoon off to go to the yard. I lifted weights five afternoons a week, coupled with good food, fresh air and a job I liked. Things got better. It was the only job in my life – 87 years – that I ever enjoyed.

When we finished our work we had 45 minutes to hang around. We put up a bar and did chin up exercises. One day Bloomie said, "Jim, do you think I could do that?" I said, "Sure, but you have to quit smoking. It's bad for you." He welcomed that, he wanted to quit and he did. When he was doing chin ups I would help Bloomie in the beginning. I'd grab him by the waist and lift him up. After a while, he didn't need me to. He was getting good!

Bloomie would never tell us when he went on vacation. We would come down, and suddenly there was a new guard there to run the laundry. He would start barking orders, and then we would line up at the door and tell him, "We want to go back to our cells." "Why?" "Just hit the power on and we will do the work. No need to holler, we don't want trouble." That would either work, or we would get sent to the Hole.

Once in a while some friends would come over to The Rock from Atlanta. One example was Carlos Ruben Santiago (1544-AZ), a short, muscular Puerto Rican. He was an army prisoner who had stabbed and killed a fellow soldier.

Carlos was mean and glared at the guards when he arrived on The Rock. So they threw him in the Hole. I asked Bloomie to get him out of there.

Carlos Santiago, 1544-AZ

Bloomie asked me, "Can you control Santiago?" I said yes, so the warden let Santiago out of the Hole. Next AM he's in the laundry. Bloomie is talking and showing Santiago his job. Santiago reluctantly starts working, but I can see he is angry. So I grab him and say, "Listen! The guy went to the warden for you. Bloomie got you out when no other guard would help you. They think you're bad – I know you're not – just do the fucking work, we like this guy! You'll be walking out on the yard with us this afternoon. Straighten up!"

Soon Santiago was with it, which was another victory for Bloomie. But some guards didn't like Bloomie. They felt he was too good to the men.

We all liked Bloomie too much to ever hurt him or try to escape. No one could tie him up or put him on the spot like that. If anyone had any plans we would have done it when he was om vacation. Bloomie got to know each of us. He would talk about his family. I was never friendly to cops on the street or to other guards. In nine years, Bloomie was the only guard I ever had a civil conversation with.

In July 1962, "Whitey" Bulger was transferred to Leavenworth, after spending almost three years on Alcatraz. Most prisoners were happy to leave the island behind, but for Bulger, the transfer meant he had to say good-bye to Al Bloomquist; the guard who had become both his friend and – one suspects - a kind of father figure:

When we said goodbye, he said to me, "Jim, of all the men I've met on The Rock, I feel you will be the most successful and have a good life."

I was set free in 1965, and tried hard to go straight but it didn't work out. Back to robbing banks, etc. I stayed in touch with Bloomie but never said anything about my crimes. Once he called me and wanted me to go with him and his daughter Candace to Canada. I told him business prevented me from leaving. I couldn't say I was involved in a gang war.

***

The gang war that Bulger mentions took place in the southern parts of Boston in the late 1960's and early 1970's. The main participants were the Irish Winter/Hill gang and the Italian Patriarca Mafia, under the control of Gennaro "Jerry" Angiulo and his three brothers. Bulger started out as an enforcer in the Winter/Hill gang, but in the 1970's he quickly rose to the top of the hierarchy. This was partly because his boss, Howie Winter, was impressed by him having done time on Alcatraz, but also because Bulger was an unusually ruthless man who personally executed several rivals within his own gang.

The FBI's big priority in the 1970's was to take down the Italian mafia, the so-called "La Cosa Nostra". Local FBI agent John Connolly personally knew Bulger since they had both grown up in the same South Boston neighborhood, and decided to use this to enhance his career. He persuaded Bulger to feed him secret information about Jerry Angiulo and the Patriarca family. In exchange, Bulger and his Irish companions were left pretty much alone by the police on the streets of Boston. Thus, the Bulger and his Winter/Hill gang received help in fighting their biggest rivals in Boston's underworld, while the FBI (especially the ambitious Connolly), received an unlikely ally in the fight against La Cosa

Nostra.

With the help of Bulger – among other things, he provided the police with advice on where to put hidden wiretaps in the Patriarca headquarters - the FBI was able to arrest the leaders of the Italian mafia in Boston in the early 1980's.

But in the void left by the Mafia, the equally criminal and ruthless Winter/Hill gang - now with James "Whitey" Bulger at the helm - took over Boston. Connolly continued to protect Bulger in the coming years, which meant that he indirectly gave Bulger's free reins to commit several brutal murders during the 1980's:

"The FBI not only enabled Whitey to murder with impunity, the FBI helped him identify potential witnesses who might expose the relationship between Whitey and the FBI so he could murder them. John Connolly, Whitey's FBI handler, deserved everything he got, but he was not the only FBI agent who helped Whitey and enabled him to murder. The Justice Department purposely focused solely on Connolly to perpetuate the myth of one rogue agent, with a rogue supervisor named John Morris, who allowed Whitey to run wild. But there were many other FBI agents, and high officials in Washington, who knew what Whitey did and allowed it to happen. They got off easy," Kevin Cullen says.

Bulger was also helped by the fact that some people in "Southie" viewed him as a heroic figure.

"There were some people who viewed Whitey as a Robin Hood, and that had a lot to do with that Southie exceptionalism, that Southie was better than other neighborhoods, and even their gangsters were better, nobler. Truth is, Whitey did give money to people down on their luck and such. And the relative lack of street crime in Southie, always exaggerated by locals, was attributed by some to Whitey, not neighborhood cohesion. Whitey went out of his way to cultivate his image as a Robin Hood like character. He knew that meant people were less likely to talk to the cops about him," Kevin Cullen says.

Bulger has been convicted of committing eleven murders. He killed some of his victims - like 26-year-old Deborah Hussey in 1985 – with his bare hands. Hussey was the step-daughter (and sometime lover) of Bulger's close associate, Stephen "The Rifleman" Flemmi. Bulger believed Hussey knew too much about the gang's dealings and could expose them. During Bulger's trial in Boston in 2013, Flemmi testified about the brutal murder. According to Flemmi, he drove Deborah Hussey to a house on 799 East 3rd Street in "Southie", where Bulger was waiting to kill her:

"She walked into the kitchen area, Jim Bulger stepped out from behind the top of the basement stairs and he grabbed her from behind and started strangling her," Flemmi said.

"It didn't take long. She was a very fragile woman."

Once she was dead, the mobsters followed their normal post-killing routine. According to Flemmi, Bulger went upstairs to take a nap while Flemmi and another gang member dug a grave in the basement.

The following year, Bulger was involved in killing two men in a car in the middle of the open street, as he suspected that one of them - a drug dealer named Brian Halloran - was planning to testify against him. The other man who Bulger and his associate killed was a family father, who had just happened to meet Halloran in a bar:

"The murder of Michael Donahue, an innocent man who was killed because he gave a ride to someone who was shopping Whitey to the police, was hideous. Especially because Whitey and his minions smeared Donahue in death, suggesting he was a criminal, when he was a truck driver, with a wife and three kids," Kevin Cullen says.

Much of Bulger's 2013 trial centered around the exact nature of his relationship with the FBI. Bulger himself has always denied that he was an FBI informant. Kevin Cullen believes that has to do with his background:

"In Southie, there was nothing worse than an informant, which is why Whitey insists to this day that he was not an informant. You can call him a murderer and a drug dealer, but he doesn't want to be known as a snitch."

***

"I do feel that Jim wants to be known as much more than just an Al Capone-like "Mob Boss", or the guy who topped Osama Bin Laden as the FBI's Most Wanted. Everyone knows he's a world-famous gangster, but who knows how proud he is of teaching Dad how to work out with weights, and that he got him to quit smoking? He's proud that he stayed friends with someone like Dad his whole life - not blood family, not Irish Mob, but a very straight family man, a guard, of all things!"

Candace Lind Jones, 62, is the daughter of Al "Bloomie" Bloomquist, the quiet, friendly Alcatraz guard who became one of James Bulger's best friends. These days, Bulger and Jones keep in close touch:

"Here in the States, Jim is a subject of endless fascination, but to me, he is my dad's beloved friend and someone I care about very dearly. He writes me very long letters, sometimes twenty or more pages, sometimes three times a week," she tells me in an e-mail.

During the years he ruled Boston's underworld, Bulger regularly hopped on a plane to California to momentarily leave his role as a ruthless mafia boss behind. For a few days, he pampered an old man he loved with all his heart. Al Bloomquist knew nothing - or at least very little - about the brutal crimes Bulger committed back home in Boston:

I would fly out, rent a car, drive over to Marin County and take Bloomie out to dinner. We would have a nice dinner and share lots of laughs about our time in the laundry. He had a stationary bike and a rowing machine in his house. He still exercised, and didn't smoke.

On one of our last visits he was sad. He told me, "You made me so healthy, Jim, that I've outlived my wife."

Bloomie was one of the finest human beings I've ever met, in or out of prison. Kind, gentle and spiritual – one of my best friends. Later, I found out he had written a long letter to the Parole Board for me.

Bloomie was showering at 91 ½ years old when he had a heart attack. If there is a heaven, Bloomie is there.

***

Bulger's reign as arguably the most powerful mafia boss in the United States ended just before Christmas, 1994. That's when the prosecutor's office in Boston decided they had enough evidence to arrest Bulger, but before that could happen Bulger was warned by John Connolly and went on the run. His girlfriend, Catherine Greig, joined him and together they became fugitives from the law.

Lyla and Al Bloomquist in the early 1940's

One of the longest and costliest manhunts in the history of the FBI followed. Over the next 16 years, Bulger and Greig were reported to have been spotted in different places all over the world, but the couple had a miraculous ability to melt into the crowd and avoid drawing attention to themselves.

In 2011, the couple had lived for several years in Santa Monica, California, under the assumed names Charlie and Carol Gasko, when a neighbor called the FBI with an anonymous tip. On June 22, Bulger and Greig were arrested and immediately separated from each other. Bulger was later sentenced to two life sentences for, among other things, eleven murders, while Greig received a significantly lighter sentence - eight years - for having participated in and aiding his run from the law.

There is little doubt that Catherine Greig is the love of James Bulger's life. He is clearly angry that Catherine is still behind bars, when several of his closest cohorts in the Winter/Hill gang have already finished serving their sentences and are today living as free men.

Kevin Weeks, who was one of the gang's most feared enforcers and one of Bulger's closest confidantes, testified against him and was sentenced to only five years in prison. Weeks was released in 2005, and later wrote a best-selling book about his time with Bulger. Johnny Martorano was the gang's hitman, and has confessed to personally having killed at least 20 people. But, as he also agreed to testify against his former boss, Martorano only served 12 years in prison and is today a free man.

I am living with the injustice of the cruel treatment of Catherine. Thanks to a cruel prosecutor – an enigma – who refused my offer to plead guilty and accept execution, saving cost of trial in money and months. I wouldn't have made any appeals, in return for leniency for Catherine.

Catherine has no police record, she is a former school teacher and college graduate who never did drugs. She taught school and was a dental hygienist. I guess in our case, opposites attract. We were on the run for 16 years – the longest period of my entire life free of committing a felony. Catherine deserves credit, she did what the police, the prisons and my enemies couldn't. For this, she received a record prison sentence. Before that, she was held with no bail (61 years old) for one year in an isolation cell, 23 hours a day.

After a year she pleaded guilty. She was taken to court and sentenced by a judge who was programmed by Prosecutor Wyshak[4]. I suspect it was a corrupt

---

[4] Assistant U.S. attorney Fred Wyshak

deal, based on my extensive experience of buying deals. Corrupting key personnel in FBI, and other police agencies, is necessary for success in organized crime.

Catherine was sentenced to 8 years in prison, along with a 150 000 dollar fine. She was also ordered to not write a book for profit. This was a record sentence for a first offender of a crime where no violence and no money were involved. Compare the sentence with the deals given to four men in the gang – who confessed to over 50 murders in detail. I call them "The Kooperating Killers", since they act like a choir for Wyshak and say what he wants to hear. One of the lies, the other one corroborates it, which ensures a guilty verdict for the gangster and freedom for "The Konfessed Killers"[5].

Wyshaks' No 1 cooperator was John M. [Johnny Martorano], who plead guilty in detail to 20 murders, including 17-year old boy and 19-year old girl. My attorney cross-examined him and he explained each murder. For this he received a 6-month sentence for every victim.

Bulger's anger only increased in 2016, when Catherine Greig's penalty was extended by 21 months for contempt of court. This means she will now be released by the end of 2020 at the earliest:

After four years, Prosecutor Wyshak had Catherine brought back to court. He asked her, "Who helped you people on the run?" She refused to talk, so they added to her sentence. It took three years before we were allowed to even write each other!

***

Whether he wants or not, James Bulger will almost certainly go into history as the prototypical, psychopathic mafia boss. He served as an inspiration to Jack Nicholson's fictional character in the 2006 movie "The Departed", and was portrayed by Johnny Depp in the 2015 movie "Black Mass". He doesn't mention the movies in his letter to me, but, according to Bulger's old friend Frank Sprenz (1414-AZ), he very much dislikes "Black Mass":

"He is extremely upset over "Black Mass", for it is inaccurate and casts him as an AK 47-toting street thug, which is far from true. The

---

[5] Bulger misspells "cooperating" and "confessed" on purpose

star of the movie, Johnny Depp, tried to interview him in prison. Whitey told him, 'Get lost, you're not me, you'll never be me, and don't ever come back, maggot.'"

When Bulger begins his letter, he writes that it's 10.30 pm on November 25, 2016. When he ends it, several hours have gone by:

Well Jon Forsling, that's it – it's 2.15 AM. Lost myself in this letter. Good luck with your book. Alcatraz was the best prison and had the best men of any prison I did time in.

He doesn't mention any of his victims in the letter. Instead he focuses on three people who, at different times over the course of his life, made him feel wanted and accepted.

Clarence "Joe" Carnes, the dear friend who called him on his death bed.

Catherine Greig, the great love of his life, the woman who stood by him during the long and lonely years on the run.

And the Alcatraz guard - the kind and gentle Al "Bloomie" Bloomquist - who always thought so highly of him. The only time James "Whitey" Bulger expresses any regret in the letter, it is when he remembers the man who once predicted that he would live a "successful and good life":

I felt terrible when I was a fugitive, thinking of how shocked Bloomie would be to see what I had become.

1414-AZ

It's the early 90's, and a German-American family is on vacation in Denmark. Father Frank, Mother Ingrid, and their three daughters live in Vermont, but Ingrid hails from Hamburg, Germany, which leads the family to spend many summers in Europe.

"We visited Germany practically every year to spend time with her family. Denmark is only a few miles north of Hamburg, and my daughters insisted we go there to visit the Lego factory. They'd leave the factory with boxes of Legos. I heard there was a ferry from Denmark to Stockholm, but it seemed we were always short of time and kept putting the ride off," Frank Sprenz remembers many years later.

He writes me from a prison in Ohio, where he has been locked up since 1995. A question hangs in the air during our correspondence. Why, Frank, did you wind up behind bars again?

You, who seemingly had found peace and happiness after all those years on Alcatraz?

***

February 14, 1959.

A small, single-engine plane lands on a tiny, snow-covered airstrip in Colchester, Vermont. A balding man in his late twenties jumps out on the tarmac and greets the surprised airport staff.

They are unaware of the fact that the man is wanted for armed robbery, that he has stolen the plane after escaping from a jail while waiting for his trial to begin in Akron, Ohio – and that he is currently on the FBI's Ten Most Wanted list.

The man introduces himself as "Frank" and proves to be a charming character.

"He was such a nice, pleasant person. I never would have taken him for a gangster," Virginia Brink, an employee at Champlain Airport, told the Burlington Free Press afterwards.

The man pays her $15 for a month's hangar rental in advance, after which she helps him to roll the plane into the hangar. His name is Frank Lawrence Sprenz, and his modus operandi is to steal planes, rob banks – and then disappear into the clouds.

The press loved him. They called Frank "The Flying Bank Robber."

***

In early February 2016, a letter arrives in the mail. It's handwritten, and contains several clippings from newspapers like *USA Today*:

Dear Jon,

Thank you so much for your interesting letter, your address is so remarkable to me that I had to return a letter to you. Many inquiries come to me concerning Alcatraz and my personal activities; however, I answer none of them and this is a first.

Frank Sprenz is no longer a young, flying bank robber, but an old man confined to a dreary prison cell. Convicted on two counts of complicity to commit involuntary manslaughter and one count of complicity to commit aggravated burglary, Sprenz is serving a 75-year sentence as prisoner number A331700 in Grafton Correctional Institution in Grafton, Ohio. The legend of the flying bank robber faded a long time ago, but he does his best to save the few newspaper articles that still mention his name.

During our correspondence, Frank proves to be to be a funny man who willingly shares memories and anecdotes from his time on Alcatraz. He asks me questions about Sweden and wants to know about my personal life. He mostly avoids discussing sensitive subjects when it comes to himself, however. Like why he became a criminal to begin with, and how he came to be involved in the deaths of two young women.

*****

Frank Sprenz was born February 14, 1930, and grew up in Akron, Ohio. As a kid, his father Frank Sr and his mother Julia sent him to a Catholic school for boys. On his way to school one day, an incident occurred that led Frank to have his first encounter with law enforcement. He was 11 years old at the time.

I had to walk two miles to get there. My mother always gave me a dime to buy lunch with. Halfway to school one day, a group of older boys, about 12 to 14, were on the other side of the street. They called me over. Then they wanted to teach me jujitsu or judo, and I was promptly flipped upside down. My dime fell out and they took it, saying "This'll pay for your lesson." So, I lost my dime and got a bump on my head.

The next day I was going the same way, with my dime in my shirt pocket and a load of rocks in my pants pockets. When the same judo trainers saw me, they yelled "Hey, time for another lesson" and headed across the street laughing. But they were greeted with well-placed rocks and left in a hurry.

That afternoon I returned from school and the parents and older brothers of the trainers were waiting for me and called the police. Three of the boys had "whitecaps" (bandages) on their heads. The police dropped me off at my house and told me to "find another way to school". I stubbornly never changed my route and was never bothered again.

As a young man, Frank worked various jobs - car mechanic, radio technician, painter, pilot - and married a woman named Alberta Mae. But he soon turned to a life of crime and committed several bank robberies before being arrested in 1958. Frank then escaped from a jail in Akron, Ohio, by throwing hot coffee on the guards. He managed to stay on the run for over a year, and even spent a short time on the FBI's "Ten Most Wanted Criminals" list, before crash landing a stolen plane on the Yucatan Peninsula in Mexico in April 1959. Local authorities arrested him and turned Frank over to the FBI in Laredo, Texas.

An AP article from May 20, 1959, on his subsequent trial in Cincinnati, Ohio, gives an insight into Frank's background:

"A 25-year prison sentence stretches ahead for Frank L. Sprenz, 29-year-old "Flying bank robber." He pleaded guilty Wednesday to the $25,935 robbery of the First National Bank at Hamilton, Ohio, last March 2. [...] During the long flight since his escape from the Summit County jail in Akron 13 months ago, Sprenz has flitted from Toronto through a score of states, and finally into Mexico where he was caught several weeks ago. He is known to have stolen at least three planes during that time. Sprenz' divorced wife, Alberta Mae, 26, has described him as brilliant. Certainly, he's been clever. He has posed, at various times, as a college student, professional football player, a garage mechanic. He often used a toupee to hide his receding hairline. He first ran against the police when he threw rocks at another boy. He was 11 then. Later he was sent to a reformatory but walked away from the institution' honor camp. [...] Between 1952 and 1957, Sprenz drifted from one legitimate job to another, but then apparently turned to full-time crime."

Just over a month after being sentenced, Frank Sprenz was sent to Alcatraz. He arrived on June 25, 1959 and stayed there as prisoner number 1414-AZ until the prison closed on March 21, 1963. He remembers those years as being dreary, dull and monotonous:

Living under the stringent rules, inflexible routines, loneliness and the forced personality change of Alcatraz gave the prisoner bench marks for people and incidents for the rest of his life. Not to mention the spartan existence; you received a pair of Wings cigarettes on Monday, Wednesday and Friday, one double-edged razor blade on Tuesday, and you'd better produce the used one or off to D block.

On Christmas Eve the Warden passed out to each prisoner a one-pound bag of hardtack candy and five King Edward cigars. That was the extent of your luxuries. No tv, radio, magazines, newspapers. One letter sent out a month, and a sterile existence.

If people want to remember Alcatraz – it's where Jesus left his shoes.

But there were also some colorful characters in the prison, who could liven up to the mood on occasion. For instance, Frank remembers inmate Theodore Green (1180-AZ) and his evening routine:

Teddy Green was a notorious bank robber from Boston. Lights went out at 9 o'clock, and at exactly 9:30 pm Teddy would break wind. He did this faithfully every night, and it was entertainment to see if Teddy would come through.

One night, a passing ship sounded a huge blast from its foghorn at 9:30. C Block was soundless, until someone yelled: "Teddy, are you all right? That had to hurt!" All of C Block roared.

I also remember Courtney Taylor (1038-AZ), who was both a prisoner and exclusive Alcatraz lawyer. He achieved seventeen certioraris with the U.S. Supreme court, more than any other lawyer. Yet, this legal dynamo carried a tame mouse in his shirt pocket, which he fed while he ate in the dining room. He also scrounged left-over spaghetti from other plates.

Alvin "Ray" Karpis (325-AZ) lived next to me. We were on the second tier of C-block, and had an excellent view of the Golden Gate. I never tired of looking at its appeal. The bridge was supposed to be painted golden, but San Franciscans liked the primer color so much it stayed. Ray Karpis stared at the bridge for 25 years and would imagine walking across it.

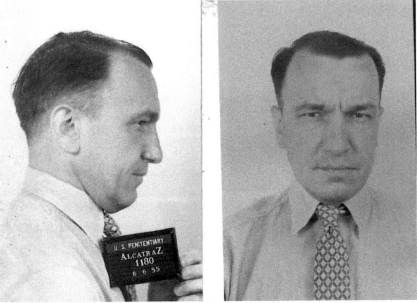

Theodore "Teddy" Green, 1180-AZ

In 1935 he was number one on the FBI:s "Ten Most Wanted" list for being the last at-large member of the "Ma" Barker gang. The Director of the FBI, J. Edgar Hoover, had been criticized for never making an arrest, and when Karpis was in New Orleans, Hoover flew there from Washington with a group of newspaper people to personally arrest him.

Karpis related to me what happened: He came out of his apartment and was getting into his brand new 1935 Plymouth Coupe when he was surrounded by a mob of agents with many .45 automatics threatening him. Then, several of the agents yelled to Hoover, who was hiding around a corner half a block away. "It's ok, Mr. Hoover, we got him." Then Hoover had Karpis by the arm and the cameras began going off.

Karpis was most upset about not enjoying his new Plymouth, and constantly told me about its powerful engine, great upholstery...I mean, he wore me out.

In another letter, Frank Sprenz talks about his involvement in the final escape attempt in the history of Alcatraz. On December 16, 1962, prisoners John Paul Scott (1403-AZ) and Darryl Lee Parker (1413-AZ) broke out of the cellhouse and managed to get down to the water. The attempt failed, but it is the only proven instance of a prisoner (Scott) managing to swim all the way to the mainland.

Scott and Parker worked in the prison kitchen and had access to the kitchen basement which was used as a storage area. For eight months they sawed on a bar with guitar strings and cleanser. I was the electrician, so I had access to emery cord and gave them a roll.

After the stubborn bar came out they had to butter themselves up to slither through the narrow opening. They got to the water undetected, inflated surgical gloves and headed toward the Golden Gate bridge, for the tide was going out. Parker made it to "Little Alcatraz", a small rock protruding above the water about a hundred yards west of Alcatraz. A guard saw him, recognized him as a prisoner, and began firing a .30 caliber carbine at Parker. The carbine held 30 rounds, with bullets spraying all around Little Alcatraz. Fortunately, the guard was a bad shot shooting in the dark, and Parker wasn't hit. The prison boat retrieved him.

Scott floated five miles to the Golden Gate bridge. By then the 50-degree water had completely overwhelmed him to the point of immobility, and he was snagged on a rock or he would have headed to Japan. A couple, necking under the bridge, saw him and notified the military police for this was a military area. At first, police thought he had jumped off the bridge as a suicide (a common occurrence), but he was in prison clothes with his name and number displayed and was soon on his way back.

John Paul Scott recovered from the ice-cold swim and went in and out of various prisons before dying in 1987. The near-successful escape - and Scott proving that it was possible for an inmate to swim to the mainland - has been seen by many as the final nail in the coffin for Alcatraz. The bad publicity that the Morris/Anglin escape generated is often cited as the single major reason why Attorney general Robert F. Kennedy decided to close the prison in March 1963.

But Frank Sprenz claims to know what motivated Kennedy – and it had to do with a tragicomic incident involving a guard named Maurice Ordway:

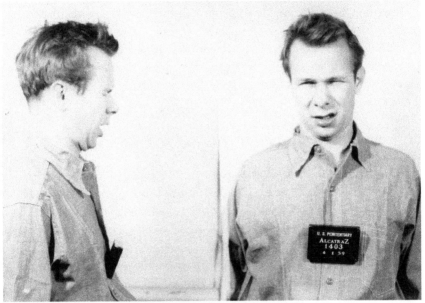

John Paul Scott, 1403-AZ

Few people know what finally sealed The Rock's ending. Lieutenant Ordway was known as "Double Tough". Ordway earned that nickname because he was being interviewed by a tv station and he was asked, "How do you survive out there, with the toughest criminals in the country?" His reply was: "Yeah, they're tough, but I'm double tough."

He was a prison guard for thirty years and was going to retire, so as a gift he was promoted to lieutenant and given a gold band to replace the gray one on his hat. He had been after that gold band for years and withdrew his retirement papers. On Alcatraz, there were three lieutenants, and they ran the place. Ordway had ascended into royalty and made a complete nuisance of his overbearing, but low IQ, character.

One day he received an anonymous tip that the Catholic priest was smuggling letters in and out for mafia bosses on Sundays when he held mass. Well, Double Tough was waiting Sunday morning for the priest, confronted him, took him to a room with two guards. They strip searched him and found nothing. Ordway knew the priest had something, and there was only one place left – the inmates favorite hiding place.

Ordway called to the prison hospital for an M.T.A (Medical Technician

Assistant). He was told, by Ordway, to search the priest's colon with a rubber gloved finger. The priest's sphincter was penetrated, and nothing was found.

The priest immediately returned to San Francisco, told the bishop about his indignity; the bishop called the high-ranking cardinal in Boston, and the cardinal called his close friend Bobby Kennedy. As attorney general, Kennedy was in charge of all the federal prisons. Being a strict Catholic, he was outraged and demanded Alcatraz be closed, which is exactly what happened. There were 190 prisoners who had to be moved to other federal prisons. The closing took a year, for only 15 to 20 were moved a month because they were so dangerous.

From 1970 to 1995, Frank Sprenz lived in freedom with his wife Ingrid and their three children. But Frank evidently had a dark side that he hid from the outside world. In the mid 90's he ran a brothel disguised as a "massage institute" in Akron, Ohio. For unknown reasons, he had a falling out with one of the prostitutes who worked for him there and was afraid she would report him to the police. On the night of September 26, 1995, Frank hired an assistant - 26-year-old Ramon Wright - who received $500 to "scare" the woman. Wright did way more than that; he set her house on fire. She escaped the flames, but two other women who were in the house at the time – Kay Westfall, 36, and Jessica Bittner, 15 – were killed. Frank pleaded innocent in the ensuing trial but was found guilty and sentenced to 35 to 75 years.

They claimed I sent some people to burn a house and murder several people, even though I was found not guilty of every charge I was indicted for. But I was found guilty of the charges given to the jury at the end of the trial, by a judge who was overheard stating "Don't worry. He's not walking out of my courtroom." She then put together charges that were unique, for I'm the only person in Ohio in prison for "complicity to involuntary manslaughter."

In March 2016, Frank surprisingly told me that he had made parole – after 21 years behind bars.

I've made parole and am going through the process, which is lengthy, of leaving. It may take another four or five months. The state doesn't understand the word "EXPEDITE".

His joy became short-lived, however. In July 2016, the Ohio Parole Board announced that it had decided to deny Frank parole. Summit County Prosecutor Sherri Bevan Walsh argued against him during a hearing:

"Frank Sprenz has not shown any remorse or taken responsibility for what happened. He is a lifelong criminal and needs to remain in prison," she said in a statement.

This meant that Frank Sprenz could have been released in July 2020 at the earliest, when he would have been 90 years old. Immediately after being denied parole, Frank wrote me a letter where he shared his disappointment:

Jon: Sort of in chock here, for after a year of going through the parole process and being approved for parole by the Parole Board, a group known as "Victims' Advocates" descended on the Parole Board and characterized me as an ex-Alcatraz thug, whose very tenure on Alcatraz made him too dangerous to be with citizens.

Five people here at Grafton have made parole this year, and Victims' Advocates have had all the paroles rescinded. The justice system in this country is overwhelmingly lopsided, with unfair judges and crusading prosecutors who twist, bend and outright disregard the law.

Frank claimed he was going to try to appeal the decision of the Parole Board. He reiterated his claim of being completely innocent of any involvement in the murder of two women back in 1995:

I was involved in this case because it's more newsworthy to prosecute a dipped-in-indelible-ink-Alcatraz-bad guy on the front pages of the newspaper. Right now, working its way through the Ohio legislature, is a bill that restricts the Parole Board to the prisoners conduct in prison and recommendations from prison staff, and they may not use Victims' Advocates, past record, prosecutor's statements, and – unless you're in for rape or murder – you only need three yes votes out of eleven, where you needed six before. The bill is retroactive, so I'll see them again with a clear conduct record and strong institutional recommendations.

***

On March 21, 1963, Frank Sprenz was one of only 27 prisoners that remained on the island when Alcatraz closed its doors for good. The media was out in full force, and the historical event was broadcast live on local television.

"Alcatraz – the grimmest symbol in North America of the hard hand of justice – is a prison no more," the *San Francisco Chronicle* eulogized. "It's just a crumbling piece of federal real estate."

The inmates boarded the prison boat *Warden Johnston and* were taken to San Francisco to be transported to other institutions.

In the last letter I received from Frank, he remembered his last day on the island. Along with the other prisoners who would soon be transferred, he waited in the Alcatraz mess hall.

Frank patiently waited for his turn to board the last ferry from Alcatraz, and to leave the desolate place that had been his home for four years.

After a while he became impatient, and finally terrified:

On that last day, we were gathered in the dining room, waiting to be shackled, with Lt. "Double Tough" Ordway in charge. As the institutions electrician I worked for Ordway and was happy to be leaving him.

When the last person on the list, Frank Weatherman, was shackled I kept looking at Ordway, for I was unchained. Guards took the others down Broadway, and out the front to a waiting bus. Finally, I asked Ordway: "Where's the chains?"

He laughed at me: "You're going nowhere. I've gotten to like you and I've volunteered to stay here and take care of the lighthouse. I'll need an electrician to help me. You'll have a nice cell in D block.

He laughed and chained me up with "I like you. But not that much." I left a trail of urine down Broadway – that's the closest I've ever come to having a stroke.

Frank Weatherman – the inmate Sprenz mentions above - was the last man to ever be transferred to Alcatraz. He arrived on December 14, 1962, as prisoner number 1576-AZ. He also happened to be the last prisoner to get off the boat in San Francisco's harbor on the day the prison closed. There he was met by the press and was asked how it felt to leave the island.

Frank Weatherman's response fittingly summed up a unique era in U.S. prison history that was now coming to an end.

He said:

"Alcatraz was never no good for nobody."

***

The last letter I received from Frank is postmarked August 19. A week later – August 26, 2016 – he suddenly died in his prison cell.

"He passed away in his sleep", Adam Kastler, Warden's Assistant at the Grafton Correctional Institution, writes in an e-mail by way of explanation.

Despite his background on the FBI's Most Wanted list, Frank's death was largely ignored by the media. The legend of "The Flying Bank Robber" had long been forgotten. The only thing that remained was an incarcerated, 86-year-old man, who dreamed of being able to spend his last days in freedom.

But that was never to be.

"I'm sorry to hear Frank Sprenz died after being denied parole. I'm convinced he had no part of that crime. A high-profile criminal was handy for some good publicity for the prosecutor," his old Alcatraz buddy, James "Whitey" Bulger (1428-AZ), writes after learning the news.

Then he adds:

"Frank was a bright guy. Now his troubles are over. May he rest in peace."

Before I learned of Frank's passing, I sent him a letter. It was returned to me, unopened, a month later. To explain why it had been returned, someone in the prison had written a single word on the envelope.

The word was:

Released.

Alcatraz Requiem

I know this will seem strange, but although Alcatraz was supposed to be for the meanest people, I meet some really nice men there. I felt more comfortable with them than I would with many politicians. – Rafael Cancel Miranda, 1163-AZ

Alcatraz was a place where they dumped you off, confined you, and forgot about you. – Jerry Clymore, 1339-AZ

The monotony was the worst part. Being in prison is incredibly boring. If someone made a movie that showed what prison is really like, nobody would watch it. – Robert Luke, 1118-AZ

San Francisco was so close to us that some nights, when the wind was just right and the cellhouse windows were open, we could hear the city life. I believe that this was all factored in as part of the Alcatraz punishment. In my book, that hit me harder than anything else they did. I just thank God that the wind was not just right that often, and that the cellhouse windows were seldom open. – Robert Schibline, 1355-AZ

Actually, it was a pretty easy place to do time. It was not a dangerous place, the worst part of it was bring locked up in your cell most of the time. There was no freedom of movement, and there were no women there of course. – William Baker, 1259-AZ

In one way, you got privacy, and I like privacy. But there was also a lot of loneliness. You'd lay there at night, trying to go to sleep, and all of a sudden, you'd hear the foghorn on a ship passing by and then you would think of them

lonesome songs that Hank Williams wrote, like "I'm so lonesome I could cry". That foghorn would make you think about it. – Charles Hopkins, 1186-AZ

I wrote a novel about Alcatraz over forty years ago, but my feelings about my writing was not good so I never attempted to publish it. The accounts in the book were serious, but mostly humorous. For there was humor in that spartan, lonely place. – Frank Sprenz, 1414-AZ

It was neither the hell-hole that the federal government wanted it to be, nor the summer camp that so many who have written about it seem to have wanted others to think it was. Why do you write a book about Alcatraz? I hope your answer is money first and to denigrate it secondly. – Harvey Carignan, 935-AZ

I have good memories of my time on Alcatraz, and look back on them with nostalgia. I wish I could spend these last days there. – James Bulger, 1428-AZ

Acknowledgements

I want to sincerely thank the following people, who have helped me in various ways:

Johnny Edwards, John Seamans and Carol Wilson at The National Archives in San Bruno, Drew Morita, Michael Esslinger, Jolene Babyak, Candace Lind Jones, Jim Gage, Kevin Cullen, George DeVincenzi, Mark DeVincenzi, Nancy DeVincenzi, Ida Luke, Peg Clymore, Andrew Brady, Ted Kudinoff, Martin Wåhlstedt, Joni Nykänen, David Widner, Ken Widner, Wendy Solis at the National Parks Service, and Michael Dyke at the US Marshals Service.

My parents Sven and Agneta Forsling, for bringing me along on their visit to Alcatraz in 1986.

My wife Jessica, who proof-read the manuscript and offered tons of encouragement and inspiration along the way. Thanks, babe. And my kids: Julie, Edward, Liv and Annie. They seem to find my interest in Alcatraz incomprehensible, but they do a fantastic job of not showing it.

– J.F.

Source material

Michael Esslinger: "Alcatraz: The definitive history of the penitentiary years" (Ocean View Publishing, 8th edition 2011)

Michael Esslinger: "Letters from Alcatraz" (Ocean View Publishing, 2008)

Alvin Karpis and Robert Livesey: "On the rock" (Little Brick Schoolhouse; Special edition 2008)

William G. Baker: "Alcatraz #1259" (CreateSpace Independent Publishing Platform, 2013)

Ann Rule: "The Want-Ad Killer" (Signet, 1983)

David Ward, Gene Kassebaum: "Alcatraz: the gangster years" (University of California Press, 2010)

George DeVincenzi: "Murders on Alcatraz" (The Rock, 2014)

Robert Victor Luke: "Entombed in Alcatraz" (Robert Victor Luke, 2011)

Jim Quillen "Alcatraz from inside" (Golden Gate Natl Park Assn, 1991)

Jolene Babyak: "Breaking the rock" (Ariel Vamp Press, 2001)

J. Campbell Bruce: "Escape from Alcatraz" (Ten Speed Press, 1963)

Don DeNevi: "Riddle of the rock" (Prometheus Books, 1991)

Darwin Coon: "Alcatraz: The true end of the line" (New Desmas Press, 2002)

Charles Hopkins: "Hard Time" (unpublished)

Kevin Cullen and Shelley Murphy: "Whitey Bulger: America's Most Wanted Gangster and the Manhunt That Brought Him to Justice" (W. W. Norton & Company, 2013)

Photograph credits: National Archives at San Bruno (Alcatraz mugshots), Minnesota Department of Corrections (Harvey Carignan), Ohio Department of Corrections (Frank Sprenz), US Marshals Services (Wanted poster for Morris and the Anglin brothers), the Clymore family, the DeVincenzi family, Frank Sprenz, Candace Lind Jones (Al and Lyla Bloomquist), the author (pictures of Bob Luke, George DeVincenzi and Michael Dyke, various pictures from Alcatraz). Cover photo by the author.

ABOUT THE AUTHOR

Jon Forsling is a freelance journalist. He worked for many years at *Aftonbladet*, the largest daily newspaper in Scandinavia. In the early 2000's he lived in Augusta, Georgia, where he worked at the *Augusta Chronicle*. He lives in Västerås, Sweden, with his wife and four kids.